Leg

Tw

ALSO BY MARK HAMPTON

Mark Hampton on Decorating

Legendary Decorators
of the
Twentieth Century

WRITTEN AND ILLUSTRATED BY

Mark Hampton

Doubleday

NEW YORK LONDON TORONTO
SYDNEY AUCKLAND

FRONTIS: *Tad Morgan's Detroit library for Mr. and Mrs. Henry Ford contained superb furniture and pictures spanning two centuries, from paneling by Grinling Gibbons to the Degas over the mantel.*

PUBLISHED BY DOUBLEDAY
a division of
Bantam Doubleday Dell Publishing Group, Inc.
666 Fifth Avenue, New York, New York 10103

DOUBLEDAY and the portrayal of an anchor
with a dolphin are trademarks of Doubleday, a division of
Bantam Doubleday Dell Publishing Group, Inc.

Book design by Marysarah Quinn

Library of Congress Cataloging-in-Publication Data
Hampton, Mark
Legendary decorators of the twentieth century / Mark Hampton. —
1st ed.
p.   cm.
1. Interior decoration—United States—History—20th century.
2. Interior decorators—United States—Biography. I. Title.
NK2004.H36   1992
747.213′09′04—dc20   91-28986
CIP

ISBN 0-385-26361-9

For Duane

Contents

Legendary Decorators
of the
Twentieth Century

Elsie de Wolfe

W HEN ELSIE DE WOLFE SAID, "I WAS THE FIRST interior decorator," and as far as I can tell, she said it pretty often, she was perhaps letting her ego run away with her. No one can pinpoint that first upholsterer who imposed his own taste on his customer, but we all know that long before Elsie there were shops and showrooms and studios that provided rooms "en suite" for rich people who wanted to decorate. Sometimes they sold paintings and porcelains along with the furniture and carpets. Sometimes they were instructed by the great architects of the time. In the eighteenth century, for instance, the interiors of Robert Adam, familiar to us all, were conceived in a breathtaking entirety. "From doorknobs to watch fobs," as I once heard a lecturer say, Adam would tackle any design problem. His carpets matched the plasterwork ceilings overhead; the motifs on the furniture echoed

In what Elsie called a Louis XVI bedroom, she mixed colors and styles in a light, free way. Her early love of chintz was distinctive.

those of the hardware and the architectural trim; the materials used to curtain the windows carried out the color schemes of the wall painting and the upholstery. This certainly amounts to interior decoration.

By the time that Napoleon and Josephine planned the remodeling of the interiors at Malmaison, there existed a company in Paris, Percier and Fontaine, equipped to render drawings of great refinement, showing in every detail what the proprietors of the firm intended to execute for their clients. At Malmaison, an example of the collaboration between client and designer still exists to prove that Elsie, whether she liked it or not, had the same problem with regard to Percier and Fontaine that Columbus had with the Vikings. But first interior decorator she will always remain.

Prior to the twentieth century the great rooms that were professionally planned were usually designed according to a taste and a style that we would all associate with a particular period; in fact they were what we call "period rooms," reflecting the exact style of a moment in history. What *did* change in this century, having undoubtedly begun in the last century, was the attitude toward period styles. As this evolution in feelings about styles from the past occurred, there arose a point of view that had been largely ignored before, and that was the importance of idiosyncratic personal taste. The individuality factor. Style gave way to styles. Where one or two points of view may have been popular before, an enormous range of styles became acceptable. If the nineteenth century successively loved all of its revivals—Greek, Gothic, and so on—the twentieth century pulled the cork. The genie got out; anything was possible (even in one room) and it still is. Oftentimes the people who make it

Ogden Codman's design for a study in Newport for Edith Wharton shows the discipline and spareness of their taste. Codman's influence on Elsie was enormous.

possible are called interior decorators. Sometimes their work reflects their own taste; sometimes it reflects the taste of a particular client. And at best there are elements of both personalities. Unlike the past, however, there is a refreshing freedom from dogma. What makes the contemporary world of decorating and decorators so interesting is the fact that various personal points of view, imitated, absorbed, modified, and combined over the past ninety years or so, have given us a broad range of styles that is almost endless. The best of this huge span of decoration involves the interaction of decorators and clients, each group bringing to the confrontation—and confrontation it so often is—its own distinct taste and personality. The rather dried-up era of period rooms is way off in the distant past. In its present form, it is the purview of museum curators and specialized collectors who are gold mines for the dealers of the world. The

result that interests me, however, is always produced by the personal taste of someone involved, either the decorator or the client; at best, there is evidence of both. Fashion and taste are constantly shifting. Influences make their appearances and then they disappear, but usually not for long. They keep springing up again. Art historians dream of recreating a room at a specific moment, hoping to freeze it in a tour de force of split-second accuracy, but the constant changes that take place and always did in beautiful rooms make this an impossibility. Looking back over the last nine decades of interior decoration, I am continually fascinated by the vitality of some of the work that repeatedly inspires us to this day. If a vigorous inspiration passes from view for a while, it usually reappears in a new and lively way later on. We are never completely free from the influences of the past, thank goodness.

As the new era of interior decoration began to take shape, three primary ingredients emerged as the most important elements of style. Vying for importance were the taste of the designer and the taste of the client. The most exciting rooms in the world are invariably the result of the collaboration between a talented designer and the client who inspires him. Often there was (and is) a third element, a further inspiration, a sort of ghostly presence of that room or person from the past that has left a mark on the present.

Elsie de Wolfe's great inspiration was eighteenth-century France, but it took the late nineteenth century and the gloom of brownstone New York to turn her thoughts back to a lighter era. Although Queen Victoria had been dead for four years when Elsie decided that her flair for decoration warranted her departure from the stage in favor of a decorating career, the world was

This is the De Wolfe–Marbury dining room in its dark, Victorian Chippendale phase.

still a Victorian place with Victorian standards and rules as well as Victorian taste. As we all know, those standards were high and the rules were strict. Chief among the rules that applied to women was the one that stated, more or less, that nice girls didn't work. Now, Miss de Wolfe was sort of a nice girl. Her father, an émigré from Nova Scotia, was a doctor, not as lofty a calling then as it is today; still, he wasn't in the retail trade, which, according to Edith Wharton, was an area of enterprise that *absolutely* prevented its practitioners from entering real society. The first career Elsie chose was acting. The distinction between showgirls and actresses was somewhat blurred; nevertheless, Elsie hit the stage without tarring and feathering herself socially. There was no doubt that she already possessed unmistakable and undeniable taste. Her clothes were usually the most memorable part of the productions in which she appeared, and the house near Gramercy Park that she shared with Elisabeth Marbury was an ever changing scene of new and enlightened decoration. In addition to her taste and style, Elsie also had a blinding ambition to succeed in the world. And, of course, she did just that.

Since dark velvets, heavy fringes, and densely patterned carpets from the 1880s are back in fashion today, it is perhaps worth being reminded of the fact that dark, heavy interiors were precisely what drove Miss de Wolfe crazy. In the little Victorian house in Irving Place, she began by painting the dining-room chairs an antique French white. Gradually, the whole room was changed into a pastiche of Louis XVI France. The atmosphere was admittedly at odds with the architecture of the house (not the last time that an interior decorator caused *that* to happen). It was so appealing and so new-looking to everyone who saw

The same room, moving toward the light with the aid of white paint and a romantic vision of Louis XVI and Marie Antoinette.

it, however, that even the august Stanford White fell for its charms. His confidence in her taste and ability was great enough for him to urge the founders of the newly formed Colony Club to hire her to decorate the building he was designing for them on Madison Avenue. This was around 1905. The interiors that Elsie created are a seminal part of the history of twentieth-century decorating in America. Cool and uncluttered, they fall into roughly two categories—some with a light, neoclassical quality derived from the period of Louis XVI and other, less

important areas influenced by the taste of eighteenth-century colonial America. In both areas, Elsie had a terrific mentor, the architect-decorator Ogden Codman, a wellborn New Englander with marvelous scholarly and snobbishly sure taste. A little later on, he and Elsie remodeled two Manhattan brownstones in a brilliant fashion based on the rules of late eighteenth-century French architecture. The finished houses exhibit a deftly balanced integration of architecture and decoration. With her typical bravura, Elsie claimed most of the credit. Never one to ignore the possibilities for self-promotion, her career always came first. She and Codman remained friends, however, and eventually they both settled in France, the source of their greatest inspiration. Elsie's world there was complex: part business always, it was also frantically social. Her house at Versailles (I should say "their" house, since Marbury and Miss Anne Morgan were part owners of it, too) was the setting for constant entertaining. A great glassed-in party room was added across the back. During World War I she was, like her friend Edith Wharton, a devoted and active volunteer in the nursing corps. The Villa Trianon and the Paris apartment, with its fabled mirrored bath sitting room, were never quiet.

In an era still preoccupied with opulence, Elsie's stricter taste possessed an almost puritanical discipline that was definitely the wave of the future. The blithe unpretentiousness of her early style was epitomized by the charming engravings of French scenes of gardens and architecture that she hung everywhere. Always light and airy, these rooms were notably understated. Simple curtains and restrained trimmings against orderly paneled walls painted in pale colors were a remarkable change from the ponderous decoration of the times. Most often painted

In its last phase, Elsie's Irving Place dining room was totally subjected to her revolutionary lightening. The quality of the decoration was improving as she went along.

or in natural wood finishes, the furniture was rarely gilded but, if so, the gold was soft and old, in contrast to the brilliantly flashy gilding popular then. Her aim was, at that time, to create a romantic mood of eighteenth-century France.

It is fascinating to return to Elsie's first years as a decorator and to trace the steps leading to her early, correct-looking French style. A look at the redecoration over time of the dining room in her Irving Place house shows how it all started. In the 1890s, while still in its brief, cozy-corner period, it had dark striped wallpaper, dark woodwork, English chairs, a gas chandelier, and a Victorian mantel, no doubt original to the house. Typical of the time, plates were hung all over the walls. In 1898 the wood-work was painted white, although the fireplace and the wallpaper remained. At the same time the addition of white-painted Louis XVI-style caned chairs, along with the removal of the chandelier and the plates, gave this phase a distinctly new look. Mirrored panels with sconces attached to them provided a slightly architectural touch to the wall decoration. A bust of Marie Antoinette sitting on the Victorian mantel, although a bit uncomfortable, helped too. A few years later an old French mantel was installed, the wallpaper was stripped away, and mirrored panels were set in around the doors. The heavy cloth was whisked off the equally heavy table, which was now painted antique white as well. The walls became off-white and a pair of Louis XVI console tables were placed under the side mirrors. An even better bust of Marie Antoinette was found for the mantel, and over it hung one of a set of large Mennoyer drawings that were to follow Elsie around for years to come.

While this was going on, Codman was doing the upstairs rooms at the Breakers, the gargantuan cottage that Richard Morris Hunt was building for the Cornelius Vanderbilts on the seaside in Newport. The main-floor rooms, astonishing for their gross proportions and decorations, were done by Allard & Cie, a Paris firm already working for dozens of Americans. Codman hated the nouveaux riches. Everything about the Breakers is

The facade of one of the Codman–De Wolfe brownstone renovations is a clear expression of their devotion to the example set in eighteenth-century France.

nouveau riche, except for the Codman rooms upstairs (and one tiny withdrawing room paneled in eighteenth-century boiseries that looks like a place where the women went to powder their noses or their wigs or something). It is easy to imagine "the clever young Boston architect," as one of his relations called him, steaming huffily past the twenty-four-carat gold tables and chairs being delivered downstairs, to install his more suitable painted French bedsteads covered in chintz that were to reside overhead.

In 1897, Codman, perhaps inspired by the atrocities of taste he had witnessed, coauthored a book with Edith Wharton entitled *The Decoration of Houses*. In it, the Codman-Wharton rules of taste and suitability were rather pedantically laid down. Their frame of reference was scholarly and historical. It was the first book for both of them and, like Elsie, Mrs. Wharton took more credit than Codman thought fair. Although they quarreled, they, too, remained friends; in fact, they *all* remained friends, and years later, when the three of them were living in their own houses in France, they continued to see one another. Their shared passion for houses and the things that went into them could perhaps be said to equal (if not exceed) their passion for human beings.

Bernard Berenson, another American expatriate, visited Mrs. Wharton every year at Christmastime. When he was in Paris, he usually went to one or another of Elsie's famous parties at her Villa Trianon. Often he spent the weekend, remarking in letters on how much he loved the exquisite femininity of Elsie's taste. These four aesthetes, De Wolfe, Codman, Wharton, and Berenson, had all fled an America whose vulgarity they could no longer stand. They were house-lovers as well. Although different in so many ways, they shared a patrician aesthetic that

The entrance hall of the renovated brownstone was transformed both by architecture and by decorating, in that order.

typified the new wave of American taste that would have such a profound effect on the history of interior decoration. Growing up at the height of Victorian excess, albeit in remarkably contrasting worlds in New York and Boston, they chose instead to live in houses that reflected a highly informed knowledge of the past, surrounded by collections of genuine things arranged in ways that did not brand them as provincial vulgarians. The emphasis was on an atmosphere of restraint and connoisseurship without the sacrifice of chic and luxury. It was a snobbish point of view and it paved the way for a new movement in decorating that lent legitimacy to its practitioners and their clients. As is always the case with successful decorating styles, this new outlook allowed people to live in surroundings that they considered reflections of what they were really like. It sounds phony, but how like human nature to invent a self grander than the real one.

Elsie was a bit phony, too, I suppose, or maybe one should say that she was simply obsessed with material things. She even considered that she herself should be cared for in a covetous way, much as you would treat a precious object. All the yoga and dieting and plastic surgery are well known. But after all, to borrow her phrase, she never set out to be Mother Teresa, and if some set out to save the poor, Elsie set out to save the rich. She was, one could say, obsessed by the idea of money and style. Although it is always said that her early commission for Henry Clay Frick made her rich, she seems to have fretted about money and her blessed percentage until her dying day. Billy Baldwin once told of escorting her home from an art exhibition when he was a young decorator in New York. At the exhibition, Elsie had noticed Billy advising a friend on the wisdom of buying one of the paintings. "How much will your commission be on that picture?" said Elsie. Billy replied that he didn't suppose he'd get one. "Don't *ever* pass up the chance to collect on something you sell!" That was her advice. She meant it, too.

During World War II, when Elsie and her husband, Sir Charles Mendl, lived in what she called the ugliest house in Beverly Hills, her style became less eighteenth-century French and more what can only be called "Venetian party theme." In the absence of real architectural backgrounds against which real society could live and play, she contented herself with mirrors and blackamoors and tented ceilings. Her great discovery, Tony Duquette, produced furniture and objects of an extravagant and ephemeral quality that seemed to convey the message that, like the war, Elsie's presence in California wouldn't go on forever. At the end of her life, she did what she had done in Irving Place. She painted all the furniture, mirrored walls to confuse the difficult problem of unsympathetic architecture, called the florist, and prepared herself to receive her guests. Miraculously, she lived to return to Versailles and reopen her beloved Villa Trianon. Shortly thereafter, in 1950, she died, at the age of eighty-five. For at least fifty years she had been the most renowned decorator in Europe and America. Her record has never been broken, and her influence has never been equaled.

Elsie Cobb Wilson

I DON'T KNOW HOW MANY ELSIES THERE WERE in the decorating world, but there were certainly two of them, and the second one came along almost immediately after the first. Elsie Cobb Wilson, another very good decorator and a great success, was born in 1877 (twelve years after Elsie de Wolfe) in Washington, D.C. She was beautiful, she could draw very well, and she was loads of fun. Brooke Astor recently reminisced about Mrs. Wilson, who worked for her parents, and said, "Of *course* she was *fun*. Otherwise my mother would never have been able to work with her!"

Her sister was Mrs. Cornelius Bliss, who was not only a good sister but also a great client. Mr. Bliss lent Miss Cobb money to go to the Parsons School where she met William Odom, a teacher and connoisseur and a great friend of Mr.

The Bliss entrance hall on Fifth Avenue had all the strict discipline of the early work of Elsie de Wolfe. Elsie Cobb Wilson was even more sedate.

19

Parsons. He became a helpful adviser and friend to Miss Cobb. Her first job was with a Miss Swift, and Elsie hated it. Her niece Eliza tells the story that Miss Cobb wrote two letters, one to Miss Swift dealing with a bit of business and the other to a friend saying how much she disliked working for Miss Swift. The envelopes were switched inadvertently; they reached the wrong destinations, and Miss Cobb was fired. As a result, Elsie struck out on her own with a little business in Washington. This, by the way, required another small loan from Mr. Bliss. Business must have been good, because by the end of World War I she had an office in New York as well. On top of that, she had been able to get away to work in a canteen in France during the war.

Somewhere during all this, she married Mr. Wilson, but that didn't last long. She was really made for work. The rooms she did for the Blisses in their big Fifth Avenue apartment and their even bigger Long Island house (where Rudolph Valentino worked in the stables as a groom) were decorated in varying degrees of formality according to their use. The children's sitting room in New York is my favorite example of the hierarchy of furniture, artwork, and architectural backgrounds in a house of this sort. The walls were finished in panels of applied moldings rather than in the more elaborate type of paneling used elsewhere in the apartment. The carpet was plain; beautiful oriental rugs were used in the other rooms. The pictures on the walls were Audubon prints—nice-looking and very educational. And the antique pieces, a few chairs and a chest of drawers, were very simple Italian. All of it was cozy without being overdone. Nothing was too rich. It had an appropriate look of comfort and refinement without being obvious. All of these qualities were clearly of concern to Mrs. Wilson.

Filled with Elsie's favorite, graceful mixture of styles, this Palm Beach loggia has none of the stuffy heaviness one associates with the place and the period.

The curtains in Elsie Cobb Wilson's rooms rarely had valances. In fact they were often made of a plain material (silk taffeta was a favorite) and they were usually darker in tone than the walls. The arrangement of the furniture always left space for other chairs to be drawn up. The groups of seating furniture stood ready to accommodate three or four people, not the ten or twelve that we often allow for nowadays. There were, however, in Mrs. Wilson's rooms (as there always were in Elsie de Wolfe's rooms as well) numerous chairs arranged around the edges that could be drawn up when and where needed. The visual effect of this type of arrangement gave the rooms the appearance of being planned for the comfort of one or two people rather than looking as though their only function was as a background for a huge party of people. Different from today. One other design element of these rooms that should be mentioned, especially in light of Mrs. Wilson's future discovery, is the strong presence of symmetry in nearly every direction you look, and the lack of clutter. These carefully studied arrangements of tables or consoles or bookcases and the inevitable pair of chairs helped to fill the large rooms of the era. They also provided the pull-up chairs central to the comfort and flexibility of the rooms. This method of arrangement also had a profound effect on a young assistant who went to work for Mrs. Wilson and who went on to great fame.

Eleanor Brown is one of the great figures of American decorating, and as a young divorcee in the twenties, she went to work in the New York office of Elsie Cobb Wilson. It would be fascinating to know what they were like together. About thirteen years apart in age, they were opposite personality types. Mrs. Wilson was high-strung and somewhat flighty. Mrs. Brown was always the embodiment of calm, disciplined behavior. But Mrs. Brown (or Mrs. McMillen, as she was called in those days) had more far-ranging taste. There is no way of knowing now what they did together. Mrs. Wilson married again—this time to Major General Louis Little. They spent a lot of time in the Orient, where she decorated our embassies in Peking and Tokyo, so Mrs. McMillen must have had plenty to do in the office back home. There is a photograph of a beautiful loggia of a house in Palm Beach decorated by Elsie Cobb Wilson that I like to think shows the hand of Eleanor McMillen. It is Italianate with a Tuscan vaulted ceiling, stone walls, and stone floors. What gives the room such an unusually appealing mood for the style and the time (the twenties), when similar houses were decorated in a heavy Mediterranean mood, is its mixture of furniture, which is generously arranged in intricate groupings filling what is a very large space in an exceedingly casual and inviting way. There were lightly scaled French Provincial chairs with fat seat cushions and splat backs, Queen Anne side chairs, a Venetian sofa covered in chintz, painted canework Louis XV chairs, Louis XIV high-backed open-arm chairs, and even four Italian neoclassical wheel-backed chairs around a bridge table.

〜

The collection of tables and chests in the room includes a Venetian commode or two, a marble-topped table with a wrought-iron base, and English, French, and Italian nesting tables and consoles and end tables from the eighteenth and nineteenth centuries. Many of these are arranged formally around the walls. A profusion of orchids and citrus trees in pots and large wooden tubs completes the atmosphere of a comfortable, luxurious room

that does not look severe on the one hand or overly rich on the other.

If Mrs. Wilson's rooms could be called a little bit puritanical, Eleanor McMillen's rooms always showed a more unabashed love of decoration, and what's more, Mrs. McMillen, or Mrs.

Brown as she was known for at least fifty years, maintained throughout her long career a thoroughgoing love of many different decorative styles that allowed her to work in the broadest range of any decorator probably ever. That Elsie Cobb Wilson worked in a narrow, stricter range of rather austere taste cannot be said to be wrong. It is simply what she did, and she did it at a time when it was new and even fresh. She was certainly an important part of the history of American taste and its unique blend, in the twentieth century, of the European tradition and the old-fashioned Yankee discipline that is basic to our best taste.

In her sister's Long Island sun room, Elsie used a Rose Cumming chintz and the French and Italian furniture she mixed into most of her rooms.

Ruby Ross Wood

 NE OF THE MOST ELUSIVE PERSONALITIES IN this whole array of interesting characters is Ruby Ross Wood. Billy Baldwin, who worked for and with her for fifteen years, always spoke and wrote of her in tones of the greatest respect. He adored her and held her in obvious high regard, and Billy was not stuffy himself. Where Mrs. Wood was concerned, there seems to have been no horsing around. One woman who remembers her describes her as the most intelligent one of the entire decorating world. Another, who worked as an editor at Condé Nast, remembers her as completely oblivious to how she looked—untidy yet voluptuous. One thing is without a doubt: she was held in the highest possible esteem by all of the people who ever wrote about her. And she was a great decorator.

She was born in Monticello, Georgia, in 1880, three years

The Woolcott Blairs' Palm Beach drawing room illustrated the Ruby Ross Wood skill at combining sleekness with a feeling of up-to-the-minute feminine chic.

after Elsie Cobb Wilson. Before she left home she had become a journalist, and she must have been good, because by the time she was about thirty years old she was in New York writing articles for Theodore Dreiser's *Delineator* magazine under the name of Elsie de Wolfe. In 1913 she wrote Elsie's book, *The House in Good Taste.* The following year she wrote a book of her own with the frightful title *The Honest House.* At about the same time she went to work in Philadelphia for Wanamaker's, a store that pioneered in interior decorating. A few years later she was back in New York running the fancy decorating shop at Wanamaker's called Au Quatrième (in case you wondered how French and English furniture compared in those days). Somewhere along here, she had been married and divorced.

In the twenties, Ruby Ross Goodenough, as she was briefly known, married Chalmers Wood, a good-looking, prosperous man whose loves included Ruby (to whom he was always devoted) and horses—for hunting, not for racing. He made enough money for them to live very well. Their Delano & Aldrich house in Long Island was a gem of American taste of the time. In the same decade Ruby opened her own decorating business. Her work began to be published in *House & Garden* shortly thereafter.

From the start, the rooms that were decorated by Ruby Ross Wood showed a combination of elements that distinguished them from the increasingly European-looking work of Elsie de Wolfe, who had a great influence on her style, and the more severely conservative designs of Elsie Cobb Wilson. If one of the Elsies aimed at creating a European mood and the other one strove to remain more American and puritanical, then Ruby can, I think, be said to have found the unique middle ground that has ever since characterized the best of American decoration. I

When Brooke Astor was Mrs. Charles H. Marshall, her Gracie Square drawing room was blue and white and French in an uncluttered way typical of Ruby.

guess you could say that she had the chic that, although actually rare, is so urgently hoped for by most decorators. The rooms she decorated in the twenties contained furniture from all over England and Europe, but it was combined with a sense of collecting and freedom that made a dramatic impression, and it was this feeling of drama and refined taste that gave her rooms an atmosphere that was free of the showiness of Elsie de Wolfe's rooms on the one hand and the stiffness and perhaps even impersonality of Elsie Cobb Wilson's on the other. To this formidable talent there was the added gift of being a great colorist. This is perhaps where her voluptuous side was most apparent. Here are a few examples of her early color schemes: gray-green walls with rose and yellow silk (two combined plain silks); yellow, apricot, rose, and green damask and off-white; or an antique wallpaper in grey, pink, and brown with old needlepoint chair seats and an old needlepoint carpet; or, in a house in Palm Beach, yellow-green walls, printed linen curtains with a turquoise ground, old red velvet, and terra-cotta. These schemes, from the twenties, were based on muted, old materials or old-looking materials. But they were not what we call dull. At the outset of her career, her own house in Forest Hills had one room furnished with antique oriental carpets and painted wall panels. The walls were dark grey and the upholstery was orange velvet. The furniture was seventeenth-century English. With all of her love of color, she had, throughout her thirty-year career, an extremely subtle and sophisticated point of view about white and its unlimited number of shades. She wrote of her own bedroom in the twenties with a mauve Aubusson sprinkled with white stars. On this carpet stood a white bed with gold swans on its posts, the two at the head holding an old white lace shawl in their beaks. The walls and ceiling were pink and the curtains were silver gauze. Imagine!

Possessing a great deal of chic, as she did, Mrs. Wood changed with the times, without ever losing her sense of understatement. In fact, she became more understated as the years went along. The appearance of Billy Baldwin in her life reinforced this tendency. Billy wrote often about her, always with

The future style of Billy Baldwin is everywhere apparent in this forties room in a Bermuda house. The Margaret Owen materials were a standard element from that moment through the next three decades.

a charming touch of awe in his tone. Both great snobs, like an awful lot of decorators, they fell into each other's arms, so to speak, from their first meeting in Baltimore in the early thirties. Mrs. Wood was at a great party in a house Billy had decorated. It was very chilly and Mrs. Wood, who was always cold, had left her raincoat on, not the act of one lacking confidence. Billy's idols at that time were Elsie de Wolfe, Syrie Maugham, and Frances Elkins. To that list he seems to have made the permanent addition of Mrs. Wood. When he went to work for her in 1935, she was at the height of her career. Her office was in the process of decorating the new house in Palm Beach designed by Maurice Fatio for Mr. and Mrs. Woolcott Blair. All the subtleties of both the Fatio and the Wood styles are apparent in this house. The other striking aspects of its beauty depended greatly on the stylish thirties and the great taste of Mrs. Blair herself, whose other decorator was Mrs. Maugham. One of the stories surrounding this project is of Mrs. Wood kneading and twisting the new hides of leather for the drawing-room chairs to make them soft and pliable. This room was a terrific example of thirties taste without in any way conveying a hint of the luxury-liner look that one thinks of in conjunction with the period. The huge living room, which formed the cross bar of the H-shaped house, had five arched windows on each of its long walls. These windows could be lowered into the ground, allowing the room to be open on both sides. The arrangement of the furniture was strict and uncluttered. The covers consisted of an off-white textured material from Sweden, tan leather piped in cream, and the Elsie de Wolfe leopard chintz. Tubs of four-foot-tall white lily plants stood against the buff-colored walls. The floor was paved with old Cuban marble squares the color of parchment. There

This very well bred–looking bedroom was decorated sixty-five years ago with clear influences from Elsie de Wolfe. Count the number of periods represented.

was a pair of Georgian pine cabinets. The walls were bare and nearly pictureless. We hear about "timeless chic." This was it.

For the next fifteen years, until her death in 1950, Billy worked for Mrs. Wood. He described her as "exceedingly frank, direct, not given to flattery and very easily bored." A little bit intimidating, it would seem, but the compatibility of their styles is borne out by the consistency of the work that Billy began there and continued to do after her death.

Another interesting fact about Mrs. Wood is her penchant for changing apartments within the building where she and her husband lived, 277 Park Avenue, a huge apartment house (now replaced by an office building) built around a central courtyard. In the days of low rents, it was easy to take different apartments as they became available. It's hard to imagine one of the great apartment buildings of Park Avenue in a relatively new condition and with low rents. But that was the case fifty years ago. One of her apartments there had white lacquered floors, brown and white Moroccan rugs, and curtains and furniture covers of blue and white striped ticking. Remarkable then. More remarkable still must have been her living room when it had deep red carpeting, red strié walls, red satin curtains, and Victorian furniture covered in claret red. The older she got, the bolder she became. There are many examples of this phenomenon. I think it has to do with great confidence. Lacking that, there can be no great drama in the twilight zone.

One of the last things of which photographs were published before her death was a house in Bermuda. The beautiful Margaret Owen tulip cotton with brilliant reds, yellows, and greens printed on an orange ground covered the principal pieces of the living room. Parsons tables were used as coffee tables. The precise arrangement of the furniture, a sure sign of Billy's hand, did not overwhelm the softer side of Mrs. Wood's vision. Her ability to stay on top of the times was demonstrated throughout her career. Her choice of successor was the ultimate expression of her vision. Billy continued to express her views for another twenty-five years.

Rose Cumming

ROSE CUMMING, WHOSE BIZARRE STYLE would have stood out in any era, is especially fascinating because she was, in addition to being a marvelous decorator, a colorful character and a great courtesan, the mistress of a titanically rich financier whose largesse kept her in business long after she quit decorating. Her enchanting shop, thanks to this terrific endowment, went on for years and years with practically no real business being conducted in it. The merchandise just sat there, as did Rose. But she was anything but inanimate. Given the chance, she would talk for hours on end, and her stories flowed on in an exaggerated eloquence that left you wondering what was truth and what was fiction, somewhat like her decorating. The dramatic effect was stunning, as was she. I first met her on a suffocatingly hot August afternoon in 1962, a day or so after having driven from Indiana to meet my future wife Duane, who was returning from summer school

The West Fifty-third Street drawing room of Rose Cumming captured the whimsical chinoiserie charm of a rococo pavilion in a palace garden. Her version of reality was not like anyone else's.

in Florence. The heat, combined with the torpor of August in New York, had left me feeling dull and bored. Walking up Park Avenue, I stopped in front of Rose's shop, which I had never seen before, to gaze at the arresting conglomeration of furniture, objects, and bolts of old chintz that filled her windows. Hanging in the center was a big, rusty iron chandelier, casually and rather messily draped with crystal. Whole areas of this very delicate and beautiful chandelier were devoid of any prisms or beads, while other branches were laden with too many strands, some hanging down like old cobwebs. It was covered with dust and seemed completely unsuitable for any customer. It was nevertheless divine in its weird way. Peeking past the oddities in the window, I saw a solitary, elderly figure with electrified blue hair standing out like a nimbus around her head. Finding the door around the corner, I knocked cautiously and stepped inside, to begin what turned out to be a long conversation and an even longer friendship with Rose, one of the most eccentric and original people I've ever known.

As we talked that afternoon, surrounded by the indescribable mélange of decaying furniture and bric-a-brac that filled her shop, I could not believe that anything she said was actually true. Everything about her seemed too exaggerated to be real. She described her townhouse in a rapturous way that I found highly suspect. Looking at her, it didn't seem possible that she could live in a house of the splendor she described. Here, after all, was this shop without a single customer during the hours I spent there, filled with things hard to imagine putting into usable condition, and presided over by a dotty, beautiful creature with blue hair, a shocking-pink hair ribbon, and a stream of stories that seemed preposterously farfetched. But I was enchanted.

The following year, while I was working for Albert Hadley and Mrs. Parish, I went with Albert one day looking for porcelain for a dining room they were decorating. Rose mentioned that in her house—that fabled but obscure dwelling—she had a complete service of Chinese export in the bird-and-butterfly pattern in shades of apricot and gold. Could we see it? we asked. "Some other time" was the reply, but as we left she urged us to make a date after work some evening when we could all meet at her house to see the porcelain. Still doubting the existence of this treasure-filled brownstone, we left, promising to remember to make the date as soon as possible.

A week or two later we actually succeeded in setting up a date. We were asked to arrive at eight-thirty for a drink, a rather late, odd hour but, as Albert said, "It's perfectly clear that she doesn't want her house to be seen in the daylight." That was a most astute observation on his part. When we got there, we were greeted by Rose, dressed in a cocktail dress of black embroidered lace and wearing a huge Adrian hat of black net with a lace fringe around the brim. Behind her stood the one other guest, who could only be explained as an appropriate prop. He was very handsome and, like Rose, Australian. Black candles were burning everywhere and it was apparent that the house was in need of a lot of general care. But it was, as she had promised, one of the most beautiful places I have ever seen. The dining room was on the ground floor with the pantry and kitchen in the back. Upstairs there were a small front parlor, a large drawing room, and a small back parlor, which she had made into a library. The decoration of these rooms was at once romantic and extraordinarily rich, but at the same time strange and mysterious with an almost Gothic, haunted quality, the result of Rose's having lived there alone for so many years. The dining room on the ground floor had walls covered in tiny squares of mercury-glass mirror held together with bronze rosettes and set into Louis XV painted boiserie panels that, said Rose, had belonged to Daisy Fellowes. The provenance of things was of great importance to her, as it often is to decorators and collectors. In this beautiful, mirrored room there hung a huge crystal Louis XV chandelier. There was a pair of Napoleon III boulle tables, and a large set of gilded Régence chairs, with the gilt worn almost completely off, leaving a finish of polished white gesso that resembled old ivory. The chairs were covered in ancient tobacco-brown leather. The floor was white marble. In the bay window there was a Russian child's sleigh filled with artificial flowers, a touch that only Rose could have attempted. The staircase, which was mirrored on all of its walls, creating a Piranesi-esque confusion, led up to the main drawing room, a double-size room wallpapered in eighteenth-century Chinese paper with a silvery grey background. The furniture was primarily Louis XV and very beautiful. There were a few conventional lamps, but it was lit mostly by candles and by lights hidden in cans behind the furniture and even dropped into the hot-air registers on the floor, so that the light came up through the grillwork, creating odd shadows on the walls. The covers of this lovely collection of Louis XV furniture ranged from very old leaf-green silk velvet worn nearly through, and silver-background brocades, to a more contemporary silvered leather, which sounds dreadful but which linked all the grey and silvery tones of the room. The floors were bare and rather highly polished, surprisingly enough. She adored the effect of French chairs standing around at odd angles on bare floors. Furniture placed at crazy angles was an

In what she called her mother's room, Rose indulged in her favorite shades of orchid, mauve, and purple, not an easy palette for most of us. Note the ostrich plume on the lampshade.

instantly recognizable characteristic of much of her work. Rose had very unorthodox views about everything, including how furniture should be arranged. The look of these rooms, with their bare floors and dainty little chair legs dancing around on the parquet, reminded one of turn-of-the-century paintings of interiors with Victorians dressed up in eighteenth-century garb.

In the front of the house there was a very small sitting room with a Russian chandelier and late eighteenth-century furniture. The back room, which was the library, was painted a rich, dark green, a color halfway between that of an emerald and lush summer grass. The sofa was covered in purple satin, a typical Rose touch. She loved satin and purple. A set of red lacquer chairs clashed admirably with the purple sofa. On the floor were two or three Chinese carpets in blue and yellow. You can imagine the shock of these colors—brilliant green, brilliant purple, brilliant red, and blue and yellow carpets. The ancientness of all the surfaces—the wood, the paint and the carpets—gave the room a mellow softness that was completely satisfying, without being in the least jarring.

Upstairs there were bedrooms of an equally exotic nature. The principal one had walls covered in shiny metallic, midnight-blue paper, the kind on the box of a bottle of Evening in Paris perfume. The bed was iron, draped with gauze and covered in smoky blue velvet. The carpets were old and threadbare. The curtains were silver gauze, hanging from mirrored pelmets in a twenties design that recalled Syrie Maugham. Everything dragged about two feet onto the floor. In the middle of the house was what Rose always referred to as her mother's room, decorated in shades of lilac and mauve and her famous delphinium chintz. In the center of the room stood a beautiful French bed draped in swagged and pleated orchid-colored taffeta.

Rose had great success during her career with her boldly colored chintzes, but the colors were nothing like the bold colors of our time. No shocking pink, poison green, or buttercup yellow. They were rather the colors of flowers in a Winterhalter painting. In fact, Rose herself was like a creature out of a Winterhalter. She looked like one, and she loved to surround herself with hazy, gauzy materials. She once appeared at a dinner party at Mrs. Parish's dressed in an acid-green crepe dress that trailed on the floor, many, many inches too long. She had pulled it up around her waist and tied it with a gold cord-and-tassel tieback. In her hair she wore a wreath of tiny plastic fern fronds. It's difficult to convey the effect that she made in a room filled with women in little black dresses. I remember that her arrival caused the doorman in the Parishes' building considerable alarm.

On the third floor there was a sitting room, the walls of which were decorated with prints of snakes and reptiles, all, as Rose said, of a predatory nature, with more purple and silver, and then room upon room of furniture stored away for some future period when her business would become more active. Which it did. Two of the people who were responsible for the revival of interest in Rose Cumming were Albert Hadley and Mrs. Parish.

The famous export porcelain did, in fact, exist, in a cabinet in one of the upper corridors, and it was purchased for the Parish-Hadley dining room. With the beautiful design in shades of apricot and gold, it became the dominant decorative element in a room the walls of which were painted the color of cognac.

Rose was born in Australia in 1887, and as a young woman came to New York with her two sisters. They were all creatures of great style. One of them, Dorothy, later went to live in Jamaica, where she printed materials which Rose used in her shop. The most famous one was a design of banana leaves printed in gold on white cotton. The exotic allure of gold banana leaves was right up Rose's alley. Her other sister, Eileen, was married to a celebrated doctor and teacher, Dr. Russell Cecil, and after Rose's death she took over the running of Rose's shop. It was she who helped to continue the famous line of Rose Cumming chintzes, which grew and grew into a very successful business. Rose had spent a great deal of time in England and spoke always of the great Edwardian hostesses as though they would come through the door any minute. One of her idols was the famous Millicent Sutherland, the subject of the great Sargent portrait that hung for years in the stairway of Ben Sonnenberg's house. To see that Sargent portrait and realize that she was one of Rose's ideals is to grasp immediately the ethos of Rose's glamorous, dashing style. Her preference in furniture and accessories was always for things of great beauty, but with a slightly mannered twist, which she intensified by the way in which she combined them. Yet she was never predictable. Unlike Syrie Maugham, with whom she shared many stylistic similarities, Rose worked in a style that was less clearly identifiable. She would create assemblages that were daring and surprising and indeed risky. However, she succeeded in pulling them off because she had the eye of a collector. It was her passion for oddity and beauty combined that gave her rooms their originality. Another area in which she was very much a creature of the twenties and thirties was that of drapery and trimmings. Her curtains were always elaborately festooned and pulled up and her walls draped in a theatrical way, with no thought for the rigors of maintenance and housekeeping. Practical concerns were anathema to Rose. She loved the style of Venice, particularly Venetian Louis XV pieces, which she would mix with French and English furniture of the same period and trim in a way similar to Mrs. Maugham's but more pronounced, with yards and yards of fringe. She once did a pair of Venetian sofas with

The theatrical, satiny realm of a Hollywood set seems to have governed the scheme of this room. The number of stools and the somewhat impractical approach to curtain design are typical of Rose's carefree point of view.

fringe on the backs in a bold chevron pattern that must have been uncomfortable to sit on but nevertheless gave them a wild stylishness. Rose's rooms sometimes remind one of Schiaparelli and her surreal sense of overstatement.

Where Rose was superior to most others in the field of decorating was as a colorist, the facet of her talent that enabled her to produce the beautiful chintzes that carry her name to this day. She used sapphire blue, mauve, purple, heliotrope, and orchid colors in a way that no one else would have dared attempt. She was also a great lover of old materials, an element of decorating now difficult to pursue because of their scarcity. But sixty years ago it was possible to lay your hands on any number of old brocades, velvets, and painted silks, all of which Rose used with great enthusiasm. We must not forget that McKim, Mead & White were able, oftentimes, to go to Italy and find sufficient yardage of antique Genoese velvet to upholster entire rooms—walls, furniture, and curtains—enabling them to give a room an instant atmosphere of the past. Rose liked this atmosphere of age and decay, though she would juxtapose elements of faded deterioration with shiny wall surfaces and mirrors so that the ancient quality of the materials never gave that dusty feeling of a room preserved from the past. Her rooms were definitely of the present. Exactly *what* present she was referring to was known only to Rose. That eccentric quality gave her rooms their appeal and pervaded her personality, her dress, her conversation, and her decoration. She was passionately attached to the objects she worked with. I remember, when the business in her shop was so slow that she was desperate to sell things, a couple from California came to buy a number of pieces, the sale of which was a source of enormous excitement. When I came back to her shop a few days later, one of the things she had sold them was still sitting on her desk and I remarked that I thought it was being shipped out to California. Looking at it and stroking it with her fingers—it was a beautiful blue bird made out of a semiprecious stone—she said, "Oh, I just decided I couldn't part with it so I told them it had been broken in packing." This touching example of how much she loved the objects she surrounded herself with explains the liveliness her rooms contained.

In an old-fashioned way she was a stickler for certain proprieties. I once described to her a room that I had seen in London that David Hicks had decorated for Helena Rubinstein, with the walls covered in purple tweed, the inspiration for which Helena Rubinstein had taken from a purple Balenciaga suit. Rose's eyebrows shot up and she said, "*Tweed* in the city!" She couldn't imagine anything less appropriate to her view of urban decorating. Yet, in the main, she was passionately unconventional.

Oftentimes on weekends I would go to Rose's house to help her clean. She lived in this large brownstone, completely alone, with no help. So on Saturdays we would polish floors or I would move large pieces of furniture and try to get to the high, out-of-reach places that she, at her age and by herself, was unable to do. On one of these Saturdays, another hot summer afternoon, I had gone, armed with a large bottle of Windex, to polish the walls of the famous Daisy Fellowes dining room. Rose, with her typical joie de vivre, in celebration of the newly sparkling room, insisted on going to the pantry and rummaging around for a tin of caviar, which we opened (I had never tasted it before in my life). We sat there, eating caviar and drinking scotch with no ice, another example of her anglophilia. This playful, generous quality, having a great time cleaning, eating caviar, and laughing was quintessential Rose. Her rooms, which were beautiful, mysterious, sometimes even a little weird, and full of risky decorating practices, had a wonderful quality of wit and humor.

It occurs to me that the combination of great taste and humor often gives an enduringly human quality to rooms that in the hands of a person lacking this whimsy would be theatrical and ostentatious. Rose's rooms were attractive because of her unique personality. It is this element of charm, even happiness, that gives rooms the lilt and the lift that can make them unforgettable.

Marian Hall

Y THE TIME MARIAN HALL, WHO WAS BORN IN New York City in 1896, had graduated from the Brearley School and started to work in the decorating field, the great early era of twentieth-century American decorating had become firmly established. The pieces were in place and the exciting developments of the twenties and thirties were well under way. With her partner Diane Tate, with whom she went into the decorating business after seven years as an apprentice with the prominent decorator Mrs. Buell, Miss Hall began to decorate serious rooms, apparently for serious people, in a style that resembled in many ways the work being done at the same time not only by Mrs. Buell but also by Elsie Cobb Wilson. It was a style far less flamboyant than that of Elsie de Wolfe and Ruby Ross Wood, both of whom worked in a more decorated idiom. The outstanding quality of Miss Hall's

Mr. and Mrs. Landon K. Thorne's New York drawing room was a direct descendant of the chaste style of Ogden Codman and the early Elsie de Wolfe. It was rich, formal, and full of precious French antiques.

rooms was a rather somber dignity. She possessed a terrific amount of dignity herself, which can be discerned from photographs and which was indeed the way she appeared in person. The first time I saw Miss Hall was in the late sixties, sitting on a sofa at Mrs. Parish's Christmas party, next to Mrs. Mellon Bruce, who was a beloved client of hers, and Lauder Greenway. In sharp contrast to Mrs. Bruce's brocade suit and rubies, Miss Hall's clothes were very severe, black with a single diamond pin.

She was a person who knew everybody in the correct social stratosphere of New York and she was liked by everybody. She adored her clients and they in turn adored her. They were her friends and they shared with her a love of a closed, exclusive social life which was carried on in apartments and houses of considerable beauty and old-fashioned formality. It was for this life and for these people that Miss Hall decorated. Her great inspiration was England, a country she loved, where she also spent a great deal of time. Although she was fond of French furniture and used it constantly in her work, England, as a culture and as a society, always retained her particular admiration.

In her decorating, the two styles were freely blended— sometimes in the same room, more often in the same house, where one room would be done in French furniture and the other in English. This particularly American characteristic of decoration arose, I think, because architects in the revival period after the First World War were fond of integrating French interior architecture and English interior architecture into the interiors of a single house. It was not unusual in houses and apartments to find a beautiful French paneled drawing room and a masculine, sober English paneled library. Or the reverse: a tiny jewel of a library with antique eighteenth-century boiseries and a big, cool, Georgian-style drawing room. And almost always the dining rooms were Georgian. It was houses of this sort that were the specialty of Miss Hall.

The first highly finished example of her work that I saw was the house of a friend in Old Westbury, which Miss Hall had decorated in the mid-thirties. It was luxurious but did not seem opulent. Large and Georgian in style, it was still an American version of an English country house. Its garden facade was dominated by a two-story portico, like Mount Vernon's, that could only exist in America. Inside there was a huge drawing room, two or three steps below the level of the hall, with its arched windows opening onto the portico. After several visits to the house, I remarked to the owner that I had noticed the entrance to the drawing room was not in the center of the wall, and how lucky it was that Miss Hall had found an enormous oriental carpet with a motif that was off center as well, thereby lining up more or less with the door to the room.

"But don't be so silly!" she said. "The carpet was cut up and sewn back together just for this room, with the design purposely placed off center but on axis with the entrance." Nowadays, the prices of great carpets being what they are and the concern for resale value being, alas, such a consideration, I can't imagine many people bold enough to remake a great carpet to suit their own needs. Very sporting, I thought. In every other way, the room was subdued and understated. The carpet, a beautiful faded Ushak, contained a large range of soft pinks and browns with a good deal of light blue as well. There were many pieces of English George III furniture, most of it in mahogany, and several pairs of pretty open-arm chairs, Pembroke tables, a huge bookcase, and so on. The paneling was painted and glazed a creamy, pale pink. The curtains and most of the upholstered furniture were in an extremely faded, light-colored chintz, hand-blocked and therefore muted. I imagine that the chintz, even when new, had always been very soft and pale.

Located at the end of the house, this beautiful room had windows on three sides, looking onto terraces, lawns, and gardens beyond. A pair of french windows opened onto another covered terrace. The feeling of being in a house in the country—not a farmhouse, though—was very strong in every direction you looked. The sporting pictures in their Georgian frames, good ones bought long before the current rage, appeared completely at home—on Long Island, not Derbyshire. Decorated many years before the slightly faddish, present-day mania for the English country-house style and for chintz as if it were some new phenomenon, this room, and most of Miss Hall's work, represented a real American style, one which combined our colonial taste with strong doses of eighteenth-century English and French decoration. This is a pretty traditional point of view and one that has been around a long time.

More lavish was the famous apartment done for Mr. and Mrs. Carl Schmidlapp at 834 Fifth Avenue. I call it famous because it has had a remarkable decorating history. After Mrs. Schmidlapp died, the apartment was sold to Mr. and Mrs. Watson Blair, a couple of great style and taste, who commissioned Jansen, from Paris, to decorate it during the 1960s. Then it was sold to Mr. Lachmann and redecorated by Ellen McCluskey. Recently, it was sold to Mr. and Mrs. John Gutfreund, who commissioned Thierry Despont and Henri Samuel to transform it completely into its present condition. Throughout all changes in this great duplex apartment, one element of Miss Hall's original scheme remained until the re-

Mrs. Carl Schmidlapp's Fifth Avenue bedroom was decorated in a style as much like that of late-eighteenth-century France as one could achieve without attempting to create a museumlike atmosphere.

cent renovation. It was the dining room, with its carved plaster palm trees, inspired by the Adam tearoom at Moor Park in Hertfordshire. Palm trees of this sort exist in a number of eighteenth-century English houses—Spencer House in London being a recently restored example that is both beautiful and exciting. It was not common, then or now, to see such beautiful plasterwork in American rooms. There was also an oval, Adam-period reception room that had been moved—lock, stock, and barrel—from London to the Schmidlapps' apartment. The living-room walls were lined with eighteenth-century French paneling and the furniture followed suit. It was as though Miss Hall thought every proper house should have a French room and an English room, or several of each. Her ability to combine these two styles enabled her to display a wide variety of antique furniture, the collecting of which she encouraged in her clients. These dignified and rich interiors show few traces of what we would call "trends." They are, in fact, "timeless" and it is easy to understand Miss Hall's feelings when she said, in an interview years ago, that she never liked "amusing rooms." She did not care for trendy, overly stylized decoration.

Mrs. George Garrett's French house in Washington, D.C., contained the European-influenced interiors that best illustrate Marian Hall's ability to create an atmosphere of richness and refinement in which a love of real comfort is evident. The furniture was arranged for conversation and for the comforts of entertaining that one would expect in houses of this sort. In Mrs. Garrett's white-paneled drawing room there were white damask curtains, a fantastic Aubusson carpet, and related shades of faded, rosy red and blue throughout the room. Pieces of Swedish, French, and English furniture, all from the eighteenth century, were skillfully combined to reveal the fondness, of owner and of decorator, for a variety of periods. The rooms in Mrs. Garrett's house, like all Marian Hall rooms, were luxurious without being overcrowded. The furniture was arranged in a logical way based on a firm grasp of proportion and architectural regularity. There were no quirky, crowded areas that fought the shape and design of the rooms themselves. Clutter was discouraged. Like many of her contemporaries, she banished all traces of the Victorian era. Her approach to furniture floor plans clearly illustrated her anti-Victorian bias.

Although restrained and almost severe, Miss Hall's style was not limited. In the duplex penthouse that she decorated for Dorothy Schiff, her sister-in-law, the effect was less formal and more like a country house. The second floor of the penthouse, where the dining room and the drawing room were located, was surrounded by terraces reached through arched french windows from the principal rooms. In the drawing room, Miss Hall used a cream-colored chintz with huge red flowers and green leaves at the windows and on the major pieces of upholstered furniture, in a very regular fashion, unlike, for instance, the more accidental way in which Mrs. Parish uses several different patterns in a room. By keeping to one major chintz, Mrs. Schiff's room had a restrained quality, although it was very bright and pattern-filled. It also formed an even background for the endless pieces of needlepoint that continued to appear throughout the years Mrs. Schiff, an avid needlepointer, lived there. Downstairs in the apartment, where the smaller rooms were located, the emphasis was on French furniture, rather than on the English furniture of the principal rooms upstairs. Small open-arm chairs, lovely commodes and mirrors, and pastel color schemes denoted the feminine, private side of the apartment. It was a practice of Miss Hall and of others to rely on the delicate scale of French furniture to create an intimate atmosphere in the bedrooms of houses and apartments where the major rooms were decorated in the English taste.

In the twenties, Marian Hall was young, but her style was serious and grown up, following the example of Elsie Cobb Wilson. The only visible light fixture in this view of a room decorated in mauve, copper, blue green, and eggplant is a wall sconce.

Over the years, Miss Hall's style became distinctly richer, with exquisite antique carpets more prevalent and the quality of the antiques more grand. Yet, while the rooms became richer and more beautiful, they did not become more serious. They were, in fact, less serious and somber than the rooms she had decorated in the twenties, in which solid-colored carpets and very simple curtains (as in the work of Elsie Cobb Wilson and Mrs. Buell) were the rule. Nor did her later rooms have a museum atmosphere. They were delightfully comfortable in appearance. There was an uncomplicated directness about her approach that was successful because of the high standards she applied to everything that went into her rooms. There was no great effort to "pull off" some trick of interior decorating. The rooms were simply decorated in a high level of taste, with fine-quality pieces of furniture chosen with what was clearly a great eye. The backgrounds, furthermore, were elaborately executed, giving Miss Hall's work its quality of extraordinary refinement.

Many of these rooms contained serious paintings. Unlike many decorators who find the presence of important pictures an intrusion in their own schemes, Miss Hall possessed an attitude that clearly welcomed the presence of good art in her rooms.

Finally, Marian Hall was one of the last of the generation of lady decorators who essentially worked for their friends. Her professional and private lives were completely intertwined in a world that was small and exclusive. But, because she was often in the pages of *House & Garden* magazine, her work for this rarified group of people was always accessible to the public. It set a standard that was very high and it revealed a certain taste and way of living that represented an old-fashioned world that, we now know, was in the process of vanishing. Although today we see a renewed interest in opulent decoration, the mood is very different from the opulence of Miss Hall's work, which was done for a generation of people seeking to escape Victorian heaviness, but still living in a world of huge houses, stables, and gardens, with all the trappings of the nineteenth century. They might have been terribly rich, but they were equally discreet.

Eleanor Brown/McMillen

O F ALL THE DECORATING FIRMS OF THIS CENtury, McMillen Inc. has been written about more often, photographs of its work have appeared more frequently, and the company has carried on in a continuous fashion longer than any other decorating organization. At the age of sixty-seven, McMillen has very few rivals for longevity. The genius behind it all, renowned for her own longevity, worked until she was ninety and lived another ten years beyond that. Her name was Eleanor Brown. She and her first husband, Mr. McMillen, were divorced in the twenties, about the time she started the firm of McMillen Inc. Later on she married the architect Archibald Brown. As she herself remarked, she did not consider herself one of the "ladies" who decorated. She wanted to create a *business,* based on professional standards. Therefore the firm she founded was not called Eleanor McMillen

One of the Paleys' guest rooms was an example of Natalie Davenport's interest in Victoriana before most other decorators had taken notice of it. The carpet was one of Madeleine Castaing's revivals.

but McMillen Inc. From the first, like its founder, it was serious and concerned with a large-scale view of the decorating field.

Mrs. Brown was born in 1890 in St. Louis, where her father, German-born but of Swedish descent, was the head of a large family-owned corporation engaged in the manufacture of gas ranges. With a house in town, one in the country, and a summer place in Minnesota, the Stockstroms were typical of turn-of-the-century rich Victorians whose family lives were dominated by strictly ordered hegiras from one establishment to another. Restraint, control, and formality became ingrained in the character of the young woman whose personal discipline and elegance were to leave a lasting impression on everyone who knew her—friends, clients, and employees alike. Years ago, I sat in the staggering River House drawing room of Mr. and Mrs. Diego Suarez, with its twenty-one-foot ceilings. (He was the landscape architect who, in 1914, designed the gardens of Vizcaya in Key Biscayne, Florida). This beautiful and tremendously glamorous room had been designed forty years before by Mrs. Brown and it was still practically unchanged. The effect of the silvery-blue-haired Mrs. Suarez, surrounded by her Coromandel screens, French and English furniture, pale Aubusson carpets, and calla lilies arranged by the ancient butler, was one of impressive chic. Describing Mrs. Brown, Mrs. Suarez said simply, "She has always been the most attractive person imaginable." It reminded me of Billy Baldwin's use of the word "attractive"—a term of high praise, as understated as the people of the world it described.

Mrs. Brown's early life was exceedingly correct, if not conventional. She attended a private school in St. Louis until she was old enough to be sent to a finishing school in Briarcliff, New York. In 1914 she married a man called Drury McMillen, also from St. Louis, whose engineering career took them for long periods of time to South America. Their son was born in Rio de Janeiro in 1916. But the marriage didn't last and, with the prescience that guided her throughout her long life, Mrs. Brown began to study the history of decorating at the New York School of Fine and Applied Arts, which would in 1940 be renamed the Parsons School of Design. The teacher there whose influence touched so many people and who became a preeminent force in Eleanor Brown's life was William Odom. Over several years, she studied with him, eventually doing a term in Paris. Through Odom, she began her working career as an assistant in the office of his friend Elsie Cobb Wilson, a woman thirteen years her senior, who, in the early 1920s, was a leading American decorator with offices in Washington and New York. Mrs. Wilson lived in the world of conservative, "Establishment" society. She possessed great charm, but she was also tempestuous. Once, after she stormed out of her sister's Fifth Avenue dining room during a dinner party, her brother-in-law had to leave the table, go all the way to her house, and persuade her to return. Which Elsie did, acting as though nothing had happened. But when she fought with William Odom, he retaliated in a different way. He suggested to her assistant, Eleanor, whom he had taught after all, that she go into business for herself, saying he would supply her with antique furniture from Europe. She relied completely on his taste, she told her biographer, Erica Brown, and for almost twenty years Odom shipped beautiful French and Italian furniture of the eighteenth and early nineteenth centuries to New York, where McMillen Inc. filled house after house with these examples of his highly refined eye. What William Odom liked, Eleanor Brown liked. Their relationship illustrates her capacity to place faith in the people with whom she worked, enabling them to develop into dependable, creative personalities who remained nevertheless symbiotically linked to Mrs. Brown's own taste and artistic requirements. Otherwise, McMillen as it came to exist would never have been possible.

Very soon after Mrs. Brown left Elsie Cobb Wilson to go to work on her own, serious commissions began to arrive, and two years later, in 1926, she hired the first of the brilliant women (they were almost always women) who would make McMillen so formidable. Grace Fakes was an uncompromising scholar of period design, a gifted draftsman, and a designer of immense authority. Prior to working for Mrs. Brown, she had had her own business. Her work was frequently published and now, seventy years later, the photographs show rooms of great distinction. Fakes had also been a teacher of architectural detailing at the New York School of Fine and Applied Arts. She loved everything about decoration and design, but she hated working with clients. So she was ensconced on the top floor of Mrs. Brown's East Fifty-fifth Street townhouse, where she presided over the drafting room of McMillen Inc. Few business relationships can ever have worked better than the triumvirate of Brown, Fakes, and Odom. The work they produced together was highly evolved in stylistic terms, starting with architectural details of marvelous sophistication combining no-holds-barred paneling, plasterwork, and floors. Added to Miss Fakes's ingenious background designs and Mr. Odom's steady stream of tables and chairs from Paris were Eleanor Brown's tremendous skills at arranging furniture. Where Miss Fakes favored a rather rigid look of almost period rooms, Mrs. Brown preferred to balance grandeur with a very inviting brand of comfort. McMillen rooms

The brilliant Washington hostess Oatsie Charles has lived in this Gothic Revival library designed by Grace Fakes for over thirty years. It only improves with age.

always sat well. Everyone who worked with Mrs. Brown observed that in ten minutes she could rearrange any room for the better.

Early McMillen rooms invariably contained a densely rich

conflation of old carpets, furniture from several periods, antique materials for pillows, elaborate trims on curtains, and collections of beautiful porcelains. Marvelous period wallpaper was often used as well. But these handsome rooms looked neither Victorian nor Edwardian. The voluptuous shapes and deep tufting of Victorian upholstery—design elements that have regained popularity in recent years—were stringently excised by Mrs. Brown and Miss Fakes. The greatly simplified designs for sofas and chairs they preferred to use are exactly the ones seen in Elsie de Wolfe's turn-of-the-century rooms. Even twenty-five years ago, when Robert Denning and Vincent Fourcade were festooning the skirts of Mrs. Ogden Phipps's sofas with deep fringes (and thereby starting a *big* trend in America), the ladies at McMillen scorned to use fringe on sofas, chairs, or lampshades; they considered it Victorian, reactionary, and unhealthy. Because of the long, uninterrupted leadership at McMillen, many rules became firmly established. While Albert Hadley and Mrs. Parish might love to hang mirrors over sofas, at McMillen the practice is considered incorrect. Mirrors are to be hung over tables or fireplaces. Similarly, stripes, a favorite motif of neoclassical design, were always discouraged in rooms where rococo curves prevailed. Serious historical considerations of this sort were a real concern. In the late thirties Marian Morgan joined the firm, first as a young student and later as a divorcee returning from Cincinnati. She was a rigorous proponent of accurate period styles and for over thirty years executed some of the grandest of all McMillen work. Her friends always called her Tad and she was an intense, impatient, and fascinating woman. Her famous short temper ensured a total, terrified silence in her office. Only an idiot would have risked her disapproval. She was a perfectionist with a profound love of England and Italy, where she spent time every year. Hotel managers and headwaiters invariably turned ashen when she walked through the door. She was terrific.

Tad Morgan hated to write or to draw, or to use a pencil at all. But she could focus on the details of interior decoration with a concentration greater than any I have ever seen. As a Parsons School student in France, she had bicycled from château to château, measuring windows, doors, and paneling, and she never forgot those rules of proportion. Like Grace Fakes, she trusted the past. Unlike Miss Fakes, she adored her clients and would go to extraordinary lengths to see that they got the results she thought they deserved. Understandably, her clients adored her in return. Twenty years ago, when she found a perfectly preserved royal Savonnerie carpet from the late seventeenth century for the then stupefying price of $200,000, she immediately sent it up on approval to a client for whose library it was the ideal size. It was bought without a murmur. Her judgment meant more than anyone else's.

The house that Mrs. Morgan, Mrs. Brown, and Miss Fakes decorated in Detroit for the Henry Fords all through the fifties was a landmark in the history of American decorating. The quality of the paintings, furniture, and decorations was the highest possible. More than any other American designers, McMillen, working in this vein, achieved a refinement and richness similar to that of the Paris firm Jansen, with whom they shared, quite independently, an allegiance to the same exacting standards of quality. The Henry Ford house was a marvelous Georgian Revival example of the architect John Russell Pope's work. Inside, like many American architects and decorators, McMillen deco-

For a library in a Greek Revival house in Connecticut, Natalie Davenport found a pair of tremendous mahogany bookcases from the same period, then threw in French chairs from three separate periods. The coffee table was plastic, a trend in those days.

rated the individual rooms in different periods. The design of the entrance hall, with works of art by Manet, Bonnard, and Rodin, was based on furniture and a carpet from the age of Robert Adam. The library walls were covered with Grinling Gibbons paneling (see frontispiece). The drawing room had Louis XV boiseries and superb furniture from both the Louis

XV and Louis XVI periods. Just how fine the Fords' pictures and furniture were become apparent years later at sales when the collection was dispersed for huge prices.

McMillen clients covered the map of America. Busches and Pulitzers from St. Louis, Blaffers from Houston, Fields from Chicago. Mrs. Post in Washington, Palm Beach, and New York. Doris Duke in New Jersey and Newport. Vanderbilts, Winthrops, Aldriches, and Rockefellers. And of course the indefatigable and ubiquitous Paleys.

Mrs. Russell Davenport carried out the Paley decorating done by McMillen (as distinguished from the work done for them by Jansen, Billy Baldwin, and Parish-Hadley). Natalie Davenport's mother, the very chic Mrs. Nathaniel Bowditch Potter, was a friend of Mrs. Brown's. Mrs. Potter's life was spent primarily in Boston and New York. Every summer there was an extended trip to Paris, where she bought her beautiful clothes. Forty-five years later, the elderly accountant at McMillen loved to recall Mrs. Potter's winter entrances at the Fifty-fifth Street townhouse, draped in luxurious furs. Her food, her apartment, and her parties are still the source of considerable awe to those who remember her. And while she was in Paris, Mrs. Potter always shopped with her friend William Odom. When Mrs. Davenport was twelve years old, she and her mother moved to Paris for a few years, establishing Natalie's lifelong passion for France. Growing up near Boston, in Brookline (where their cousin, John Singer Sargent, would come to lunch and draw his ravishing charcoal portraits of the ladies of the household), and in Paris, all under the guidance of her fabulous mother, the young Natalie found her own dashing style. For years she wanted to be an actress and succeeded, after acting school, in getting roles in three or four plays, one of which was a Max Reinhardt production of *A Midsummer Night's Dream,* in which she played half a tree.

Because Mrs. Davenport's first apartment in Manhattan was very attractive—this was just before World War II—a friend asked if she would decorate her apartment. Mrs. Davenport asked if she could execute the job through McMillen. Mrs. Brown, knowing Mrs. Davenport well and admiring her mother, agreed. Then came the war. With her dramatic aspirations, Natalie the actress moved to Kentucky and took over a radio program. Typically, her housing was rather more stylish than that of most other people; she lived at the Binghams', the Louisville newspaper moguls. When her employers wanted to transfer her to Chicago, she knew it was time to return to New York. Billy Baldwin offered her a job. So did *House & Garden.* But before making a decision, she talked to Mrs. Brown, who wanted to hire her too. She was the first decorator at McMillen who had not been trained at the Parsons School. Her style encompassed a wide, very sophisticated range of periods. French taste always dominated her point of view. After all, France was a second home to her. (Miss Charlotte Nolan, headmistress of Foxcroft School, which Natalie attended, had been astonished to find that the child's French was better than her English.) Mrs. Davenport knew and admired Emilio Terry, the brilliant Parisian architect, and she was fascinated by the taste of his client Charles de Beistegui. Her marvelous room in Nassau for the Paleys bore distinct traces of the Beistegui style, with its revived interest in the taste of the seventeenth century—all of those Louis XIII, Louis XIV, and Daniel Marot elements then almost unknown here. They were known in Paris, so they were known to Natalie

Davenport. So was the work of Madeleine Castaing, the French *antiquaire* and decorator whose extremely personal style also captured the imagination of Billy Baldwin, David Hicks, and Albert Hadley.

Albert Hadley spent six or seven years at McMillen. While he was there, he sat across from Mrs. Davenport and they exchanged ideas all the time. Albert has always been one of her devoted admirers, as she is of him. His resignation from McMillen was caused by an interview Mrs. Brown gave to a newspaper stating her belief that women were better decorators than men. Albert left the following day, to join Mrs. Henry Parish, with whom he would proceed to make decorating history.

Women *did* rule the roost on East Fifty-fifth Street. Even now, the firm is run by Betty Sherrill, who went to work there exactly forty years ago. Ethel Smith, partly retired now, who worked at McMillen for fifty years, is still a mentor to Mrs. Sherrill. Over their many years together, they restored the ravishing Rosedown Plantation in Louisiana, a tour de force of Louis Philippe period decoration in America, Blair House in Washington, and innumerable houses up and down the east coast of the United States. They worked for Lady Bird Johnson and Betty Ford. They tackled offices, country clubs, and showrooms. Mrs. Brown's visionary, open-minded view of the decorating profession imbued her staff with the attitude that they could do anything. Working under her august gaze, they certainly could. Dozens of her competitors tried to imitate Mrs. Brown's style, but she sailed right over them like a ship of state.

Frances Elkins

F YOU THINK ABOUT THE EVOLUTION OF THE American style of interior decoration and how it has differed from that of Europe, it seems clear that our social and political climates have had an unmistakable effect on the way American houses have looked throughout our history. There has usually been a look foreign to aristocratic taste, or should I say that aristocratic taste was foreign to our own? The idea of European style was, of course, always in the back of our minds. But the element of glamour, that highly charged and highly visible quality that few possess, has been rather rare in the realm of American taste. You can dredge up examples, but they are often exceptions. They were usually cases of someone's looking to Europe for a kind of mood that was basically not to be found here. *Or* they were looking to that hugely influential place in American life—Hollywood.

Her unerring sense of how much of the past to mix with design elements of the present gave Frances Elkins the ability to create modern classics. Her own bedroom in Monterey is just as chic as it was fifty years ago.

In Hollywood there were art directors and designers who were in touch with all the great movements in European design; many of these men were indeed European. They were marketing glamour (I'm talking about the twenties and thirties) in a way that has never been surpassed. Platinum blondes dripping in silver fox, hanging on the arms of men in white tie, and gliding across mirrorlike polished floors (what *were* those floors made of?). Or climbing out of custom-made Dusenberg convertibles. *That* was glamorous. For many of the decorators who tried to emulate that glamour, to inject some part of it into their rooms, the results were disastrous. Too glitzy, too impersonal, and simply vulgar. One notable exception to this failing was the work done by Frances Elkins (1888–1953), a Midwesterner by birth, who settled in Monterey around 1918 and who went on to become a decorator of remarkable talent and fame. Furthermore, she was the first great California decorator.

At the outset of his career, Billy Baldwin had three idols—Elsie de Wolfe, Syrie Maugham, and Frances Elkins. Elsie's work, as the years went on, became more and more European. Syrie's was of course English, with large doses of Continental flavoring, to which she added current elements of the Art Deco movement. But Frances Elkins's work was distinctly American, with, although she used European furniture a great deal of the time, a clean, fresh look that is often identified with American design. There are photographs of two rooms, one decorated by Mrs. Maugham and the other by Mrs. Elkins, which possess uncanny similarities: Syrie's own dining room in Buckinghamshire and Frances's entrance hall in the Zellerbach house in San Francisco, both done in the thirties and containing identical plaster palm-tree pilasters and console tables in the style of Jean-

Michel Frank. But while Syrie's dining room is whimsical and feminine, Frances's hallway is strict and spare. On the floor, and going up the stairway, there were Moroccan rugs woven in a geometric pattern. Although the elements were eclectic, the effect was one of totally coherent cleanness. This starched quality of crisp simplicity came to be the stamp of the Frances Elkins style. It is the quality that left such a profound mark first on Billy Baldwin and later on Michael Taylor, to name two of her most famous followers.

Without diluting my praise of Frances Elkins, I must add that she was the younger sister of the brilliant Chicago architect David Adler. If she had a tremendous influence on other decorators, it must be pointed out that her brother had an equally tremendous influence on *her*. He was six years her senior, and it was he who kept her in line, to use her daughter's words. From their youth, they traveled often in Europe. Their mother, a great beauty all of her life, loved to travel. Mr. Adler *père,* a Milwaukee clothing manufacturer, seems to have stayed home to make the money that supported the wanderlust. David Adler's prodigious talent was apparent at an early age. Even as an undergraduate at Princeton, he inspired enough confidence to be chosen to design the new building for his eating club.

After Princeton, he traveled in earnest through Europe and eventually was put through the École des Beaux-Arts by a rich uncle who lived in Glencoe, Illinois. This figure, their uncle Stonehill, helped both David and Frances over the years. David designed a big Louis XIII-style house for him overlooking Lake Michigan, and later, when Frances was divorced and living in California, he helped her finance her new decorating business.

It would be difficult to imagine a combination of qualities

better suited to a brilliant decorating career than those possessed by the young Frances Elkins. She was ahead of her time in some ways but still perfectly attuned to it in others. Her husband had dropped by the wayside; her relationship with her hugely successful brother was extraordinarily good, and she was living in California, where decorating opportunities were enormous. Years of travel in Europe had equipped her with a knowledge of the history of decoration that reinforced her own great taste. With her broad-minded outlook and her sense of fashion, she was able to view sympathetically modern trends in decorating as well as traditional styles. This is not a particularly common phenomenon.

Her love of France had produced friendships with two people who would have a lasting effect on her life and her style. One was Coco Chanel and the other was Jean-Michel Frank. Like her decorating, Frances's appearance was noteworthy. All those who remember her mention the spit curls that always fringed her forehead. And her clothes were ordered in Paris each year from Chanel. When Chanel closed down, she switched to Mainbocher, who supplied her with the simple, chic clothes she preferred all her life. After her death in 1953, a young California lawyer working on the settlement of her estate came across a bill from Mainbocher for three gingham dresses for a total of $1,800. The young lawyer called Mrs. Elkins's executor to ask if he had ever heard of Mainbocher and to check the possibility that the bill was inaccurate. Gingham dresses, said the lawyer, cost $30 in Palo Alto. Luxury that might escape the attention of ordinary eyes was what appealed to Frances Elkins.

In that respect, her philosophy resembled Jean-Michel

The strict color scheme of this dining room serves to organize Georgian, Victorian, and contemporary furniture and decorative objects into a bold and dramatic design. How could you possibly tell it was executed fifty years ago?

Frank's. Not only did he influence her decorating style; he also became a friend and the supplier of countless pieces from his shop in Paris. His hand is visible in dozens of Mrs. Elkins's rooms, yet her interpretation of the Frank style is always combined with her own sense of how things should look, a softer, more varied approach.

Her 1830 adobe house in Monterey, which she purchased in 1918 for $5,000, was one of the first expressions of her taste, and happily it is one that has survived to the present day, including its little glassed-in conservatory and courtyard garden, both of which David Adler helped to design. Today the house is a United States Historic Trust landmark. The decoration of the house is completely undated, containing all those elements that Frances Elkins fused together in her work. The range of furniture includes English and French antiques, the French pieces being of a rather provincial nature. Antique Directoire wallpaper covers the walls of the upper stair hall. Chinese carpets and objects are mixed with the French and English pieces in the large living room. The colors of the hall and living room, in a way typical of Mrs. Elkins, are closely linked, which is the controlling element that makes the two spaces, with all their diversity, appear to be so logical and so satisfying. The strong blue of the paper is repeated again and again in the carpets, porcelains, cloisonné, and materials. Yet the subtle gradations always present in old things make any possibility of monotony impossible. The careful selection and individual quality of the furniture and objects also prevent the rooms from having any hint of the commonplace. Finally, Frances Elkins, always encouraged by her brother, was driven by an unrelenting need for symmetry. So, with their highly controlled color schemes and strictly symmetrical formats, her rooms possessed a sharp clarity often lacking in other decoration. Because she loved a huge range of periods and styles, her decorating was not plagued by that arid quality many of us detect in rooms that are either too stylized or too decorated. There was, to be sure, no pretense about the "undecorated" look. Her rooms were highly thought out and highly decorated. They were just very subtle.

The master bedroom of the Monterey house was the embodiment of Frances Elkins's prophetic style. With whitewashed walls and a shaggy white cotton carpet and practically no patterns, its atmosphere was light and soft. A simple four-poster bed was painted white and canopied with white cotton fishnet. The coverlet was pale pink. What might have been a reference to Early American bed canopies was, however, thrown to the winds by heavy ball fringe trim and huge corner tassels made of the ball fringe as well. The mantel and chairs were Louis XV. The simplest possible trumeau mirror hung between plaster shell sconces of a Jean-Michel Frank type. The plaster ceiling light also bore his stamp. A clipped white fur throw on the foot of the bed added another luxurious, blond tone to the room. Its position in the history of interior decoration is more than that of just another pretty room. Its references to the time in which it was created subtly call to mind Syrie Maugham and Jean-Michel Frank. In spite of all its old-fashioned elements, it was still a room of clean, uncluttered modernity. And, finally, it was a fascinating precursor, as much of her work is, of Michael Taylor, who gave the ultimate shape to California decorating in our time. Equally close in its relationship to the work of Michael Taylor is a room she did for Mr. and Mrs. George Coleman in the forties. (Mrs. Coleman is now the Duchess of Manchester.) The motif was blue and white. Chinese porcelain, Mexican pottery, and Delft tiles, all in compatible shades, established that paradox of matched but not really matched colors and materials.

This Lake Forest powder room has all the glamour of the thirties. It is also a tour de force of design and craftsmanship, with lacquerwork and mirrors of superb quality.

A hand-blocked linen in a bold, two-dimensional pattern typified her love of strong, flat designs. The linen covering the furniture, which was almost geometric in its sharpness, was printed in the same blue and white of the strict color scheme. A white coffee table with a Miró-like design on the top added an arts-and-crafts element frequent in her work, and on one side of the tiled fireplace, in the otherwise symmetrical setting, stood a white plaster twisted floor lamp, another Frank design that later became a staple in the work of Michael Taylor.

If the people Mrs. Elkins worked for were chic, and they certainly were, her own style was every bit as stylish. The food that came out of her kitchen, prepared by her longtime cook, Clementine, was known for its excellence. Everything about her housekeeping was charged with her personal combination of old-fashioned luxury and contemporary chic, even down to the ivory-handled spoon on the bar that Syrie Maugham is said to have coveted.

Her amusing personality made her a sought-after companion by a large and interesting variety of people devoted to art and design. In addition to Frank and Chanel, her friends included Misia Sert, Syrie Maugham, and Dorothy Liebes, from whom she commissioned tremendous amounts of specially woven materials, as well as a large number of craftsmen who enabled her to produce the unique handmade pieces that always distinguished her work. They were all devoted to her, and apparently she returned their devotion.

A large sitting room she did at the University of California at Berkeley in the forties contained bleached wood and leather-covered tables, all of which were made in Monterey. Spotted cowhide rugs anchored the numerous islands of furniture in the huge space. Looking at the pictures of this room nearly fifty years later, I see nothing that looks out of date, unless one dwells with particular emphasis on animal rights. From her vantage point in California, and given her sophisticated knowledge of the design world, Frances Elkins synthesized different styles in a way that was typically American but which went beyond anything else done at the time. As a prophetess, she was unequaled. No wonder Billy Baldwin admired her; she might have been his teacher, so closely did his view of decorating seem to fit hers.

Sixty years or so ago, Mrs. Elkins began to work on a house in Lake Forest for Mr. and Mrs. Kersey Coates Reed that survived intact until recently. Photographs of its stupendous interiors appeared from time to time, always looking amazingly chic. When these marvelous interiors were about fifty years old, I was taken to see them by a daughter of Mrs. Elkins's client, who had grown up in the house. Far from being disappointed by what the passage of time had done to the place, I was simply astonished by its perfection, by the impeccable finesse with which traditional Anglo-American decoration and up-to-the-minute thirties design had been combined. It must be pointed out that the architect of this great house was Frances's brother, David Adler, who was operating at the top of his form. It was built in the period of his greatest houses: Castle Hill in Ipswich for the Cranes; the Tobin Clark masterpiece in San Mateo, to name just two. The other clear collaborator, although it is not clear exactly *how* he went about it, was Jean-Michel Frank. Whereas Castle Hill is an essay in the Queen Anne style and the Tobin Clark house is a brick and timbered Tudor affair, the Reed house is a huge, somber, Pennsylvania fieldstone house in the Georgian style consisting of a center block and large two-story flanking wings. Judging from the exterior, one might have expected to find on the inside a serious collection of Philadelphia furniture or some equally puritanical expression of colonial American taste. Nothing, however, could have been further from the cool glamour that greeted you the second you stepped into the entrance vestibule. Standing on the glassy black and white marble floor were a pair of white gessoed eagle console tables. Stamped on their undersides were the words "Malletts London," so I assume that they were made for the space. Over them hung a pair of gilt pedimented mirrors, establishing the rigid symmetry that dominated not only the house but also the work of Mrs. Elkins and her brother. Opening off each side of the vestibule were two cloakrooms, one for men and one for women. Each of these rooms (and they weren't tiny little lavatories) possessed the qualities of full-blown interior decoration at its most stylish. The men's side was Mrs. Elkins's introductory essay in the Jean-Michel Frank presence that appears here and there in the house. On a beautiful, bare parquet floor stood a pair of big leather easy chairs covered in luggage-tan leather, their backs and arms sharply squared. At their sides were low tables with plaster lamps. A pale wood table and X-legged bench occupied the wall opposite the door. Above them hung a mirror and two plaster wall lights. Over the fireplace (need one emphasize the importance of a fireplace in a cloakroom?) there was a plaster panel in relief by Alberto Giacometti. In any house of the present time, these elements would provide the decorative background of a major room. For Frances Elkins, they formed an inconceivably chic scheme for a men's loo!

Across the hall, the ladies' division was, if anything, even more stylish. The walls were laid out in a paneled design, the panels filled with mirror. Surrounding the overmantel and the dressing-table niche were mirrored glass bolection moldings in a Queen Anne design. Furniture of black lacquer and silver leaf, in designs reminiscent of some of the work of Edwin Lutyens, continued the early eighteenth-century theme of the room. The Art Moderne atmosphere that pervaded this house was not, however, ignored. The parquet of the floor was made up of black rubber tiles with polished aluminum inserts that echoed the silvery color of the mirrors. Every surface of this remarkably glamorous room sparkled with a high gloss. I have never seen a more refined finish in a room. But that, of course, was true of the entire house.

The vast cross hall, which cut through the middle of the central block of the house, continued the black and white marble floor, terminating at one end with monumental black marble columns with white Ionic capitals and bases, beyond which rose a perfectly shaped elliptical staircase. Mrs. Elkins's strict adherence to a coherent design vocabulary in the houses she decorated was as apparent here as it was in the ladies' cloakroom. The early eighteenth-century aspect of the decoration was expressed by the bluntly simple cut-glass chandelier. The modern crafts that she so loved appeared in the Moroccan runner made specially for the stairway. The Art Moderne movement crept in by way of the stair spindles, which were made of turned glass. All of this complex mixture of periods illustrates Mrs. Elkins's fearless skill.

So then you can imagine the many layers of style and design that, woven together, made up the extraordinary luxury, glamour, and chic of this American house built on the shores of Lake Michigan sixty years ago and decorated in a way that, over those years, was never outdated and today would make headlines as a new, fresh interpretation of everything that is thought to be strong, architectural, and beautiful. But there is more—the library, the guest room, and the dining room were equally remarkable. The dining room, memorable enough for its Chinese Chippendale chairs and antique Chinese wallpaper, was still firmly anchored in the twentieth century by a huge, geometric Marion Dorn carpet of dark brown wool. The guest room, with

Syrie Maugham and Jean-Michel Frank come to mind when one looks at this San Francisco hall decorated by Frances Elkins. Her approach to the same elements was as individual as each of theirs. Designers all across America still copy every single element, even the modern Italian glass vase.

its silver-leaf wallpaper and faded Samarkand carpets, had as its major decoration a spectacular pair of turned ivory poster beds in the style of the Indian Raj. The library, however, was the most boldly stylish room I have ever seen in this country. Not warm, and not cozy, but incredibly chic.

The walls were covered in squares of light tan pigskin stitched together with heavy thread. The woodwork of the room (mantel, door casings, and so on) was finely carved, eighteenth-century English pine, stripped of its paint and, consequently, pale and dry, with traces of gesso left in the carving. On the floor, another faded Samarkand carpet reinforced the effect of a room drained of its color. The sofas and armchairs of the same strapping, Jean-Michel Frank design as those in the men's cloakroom and covered in the pigskin of the walls gave the impression of modernity that existed everywhere in this otherwise classically traditional house. Finally, and almost too much for the taste of those of us who shy away from overstatement (even though we might admire it when it is achieved without vulgarity), all the books in the bookcases were jacketed in parchment dustcovers, the spines of which had cutouts to show the titles. If this sounds absurdly mannered and self-conscious, I can only say that it looked fantastic. It reminded me of a glimpse of a long corridor of stacks I had once seen in the Vatican library. For as far as the eye could see, there were rows of shelves filled with manuscripts bound in vellum and tied with natural-colored tapes. I could have been very happy in either place.

That future generations imitated Frances Elkins is perfectly clear and, given her understanding of all the elements that make up style, it is not surprising. The remarkable aspect of her influence is the fact that two of her most ardent followers—Billy Baldwin and Michael Taylor—stood out in their own time as great leaders themselves. The quality of influencing the greatest of her successors is what makes Frances Elkins one of the most interesting and most significant figures in the history of American design. Whether she was decorating for conservative rich people in the Midwest or for movie stars in Beverly Hills (Edward G.

Robinson was one of the latter category) or for Mr. and Mrs. Marshall Field in New York, she captured the look of the time with an uncanny sense of the future, on the one hand, and a clear, dignified respect for the past on the other. No other decorator did more to define the broad aspects of American taste.

Jean-Michel Frank

EVERY NOW AND THEN A CONFLUENCE OF legendary, talented people occurs in the history of any creative movement, leaving a memorable stream of influence that flows along through time in a seemingly endless way. For generations and sometimes even centuries to come, these inspired groups continue to stimulate the imaginations of others, leaving their mark on the work of those future followers who keep the legend going—who in fact *make* them legends in the first place. Jean-Michel Frank and his coterie of designers and artists—the Giacomettis, Emilio Terry, and Christian Bérard, to name the most famous of the lot—show every sign of being one of the twentieth century's most enduring sources of contemporary inspiration. Frank, of course, was the central figure in this group, and from the first appearance of his rooms and then of his shop in the Rue du Faubourg Saint-

The late-twenties drawing room designed for Charles and Marie-Laure de Noailles in Paris possesses all the qualities of Frank's extemely original style. He used scale as a way to achieve drama and surprise.

Honoré, the influence of his taste on other designers of the time was tremendous. His exquisite work has, moreover, never looked dated or passé in the more than sixty years since it first appeared. At the present moment, a new generation of designers and decorators seems to be discovering all over again the subtle chic of the Jean-Michel Frank style.

The style itself is interesting to contemplate and to describe. Possessing an "ambiguous sensuality," as Andrée Putman phrased it so aptly, the Frank style is nevertheless loaded with *un*ambiguous qualities that give it a brilliant visual clarity. Two of the most prominent of these qualities, both involving exaggeration, are the openness of the spaces, giving an almost empty look, and their subdued, nearly colorless tonality. Vast rooms do, after all, exist more often in great Paris houses and apartments than in their American counterparts. After Jean-Michel Frank got through with a room, it looked bigger than ever. His color palette ran the gamut, as Dorothy Parker once said in another context, from A to B. Most of the time, there was just one color: a creamy beige, going to white on one end of its short chromatic journey and to a golden, woody brown at the other. Above all, in these great, spacious atmospheres there was a quality of light and lightness, even though he constantly experimented (and successfully, too) with overscale. Then the "sensual ambiguities" begin to set in. The battle between luxury and simplicity, constantly fought in the world of modern design, seems to have been peacefully resolved by Frank. Without appearing to be really rich and never seeming to be the least bit vulgar, his rooms were always full of a sense of glamour and extravagance. Because the materials he favored are traditionally associated with informality, the first impression made by his rooms was an informal

If one thinks of Frank as a rigid figure, the Noailles hall surely dispels that point of view with its mixture of serious and funny details.

Frank's own workroom, like many of his interiors, was treated as a box in which geometric shapes were loosely arranged.

one. Pale and medium-toned leathers or solid textures covered huge sofas and chairs. There was, as a rule, no pattern. Frank's leatherwork was superb, not surprisingly since it was often executed by Hermès. Tables and small chairs were completely covered with it. Cartonnières designed in a manner reminiscent of the eighteenth century were faced with it and, sometimes, the entire carcass of a commode was leather-covered. Rather than looking overly masculine or officelike, Frank's delicately detailed leather pieces were precious and rich. Simple linens and silks, coarse tweeds, men's suiting materials, corduroy—all of these plain materials were used for upholstery or for curtains, always treated in the simplest way possible. The hard surfaces were usually plain as well, but in the spirit of ambiguity that pervades Frank's work, the plainness was deceptive. It did not mean that what you saw was simple; it only *looked* simple. Vellum, lacquer, shagreen, and straw, for example, were widely used, not only for covering small things but for entire walls as well. Wood, usually finished in light tones, although ebonized once in a while, was often left in a dry, sanded state that looked almost unfinished. His love of bronze is well known. Huge, polished sheets covered doors, while gnarled lamps and tables by Alberto and Diego Giacometti conveyed a rougher, more sculptural impression. In addition to the rich, dark bronze objects, there were light, primitive-looking plaster ones—urns, vases, lamps, and so on, many of them inspired by classical forms. Along with his fondness for classicism (a penchant surely intensified by his dialogues with Emilio Terry), there was a great fondness for all sorts of primitiveness, from early French and Continental examples to African tribal art. Most conventional objects and all groupings that might be called "clutter," even paintings on the walls, were banned by Frank as enemies of his minimalist state. But minimalism was not, as is so often the case nowadays, imposed on the occupants of Frank's rooms without regard to their physical comfort. There were plenty of chairs, tables, lamps, and cushions, and they were arranged in a loosely organized way, often placed at odd angles to one another, which not only allowed for easy comfort but spoke visually of a more carefree attitude than, say, that of Bauhaus rooms. Here, as usual, the difference between France and Germany was very clear.

Not that Frank was carefree. He stood apart from the time

of his early childhood. Lonely and melancholy, he was thin and fey, and spoke in an exceptionally high-pitched voice. His exotic Eastern looks were accentuated in his adult years by his severe London wardrobe, which consisted primarily of a large number of identical grey flannel suits. The tension and isolation of growing up as an oddly aesthetic child and a Jew in an anti-Semitic atmosphere intensified his melancholy turn of mind. Real disasters occurred with the death of his two brothers in World War I, which led to his father's suicide. Then, when he was still in his early twenties, his mother, already in an asylum, died. It was 1919; Frank was twenty-four. With his new financial independence, he decided to take up traveling, after which he returned to Paris, where he later chose to decorate an apartment for himself. He hired a decorator by the name of Adolphe Chanaux, who had worked with Ruhlmann, among others, in the Art Moderne movement and who had developed negative feelings about the current state of French design. Chanaux's ideas fell on sympathetic ears and Frank must have felt somehow rescued from the desperate situation that faced him, because soon he himself was designing interiors, and by the end of the twenties his brilliant but tragically short career was well under way. He was established as an outstanding light in the world of Parisian design. The shop that he and Chanaux opened in the Rue du Faubourg Saint-Honoré was filled with inspired furniture and objects, the furniture designed by Frank and the rest by the members of the group of artists who made up his circle. It was not simply a place to buy pretty things. It was the source of a new style. Frank's influence was tremendous. Two of his foreign customers, Syrie Maugham and Frances Elkins, introduced his ideas to London and to the West Coast of the United States.

With the help of her superbly talented brother, the Chicago architect David Adler, Frances Elkins spread Frank's influence over a range of houses from coast to coast. His designs became a permanent part of the decorating vocabulary of the time.

Although Frank worked in South America and the United States, where he fled the Nazis, his greatest monuments were, of course, in France. His most famous and perhaps most enduring work exists in the great Paris townhouse that belonged to the Vicomte and Vicomtesse Charles and Marie-Laure de Noailles. Unlike so many contemporary rooms of great importance which disappear, with only photographs to remind us of how they looked, these rooms have survived, albeit in an evolved state, into the present. When I went to see them in the early seventies, I had no idea what to expect. The house, a mammoth limestone *hôtel particulier* built by the vicomtesse's grandfather, is a palatial evocation of the late eighteenth century. The immense stone hall and staircase convey an impression of Victorian, baronial grandeur that leaves little room for thoughts of twentieth-century modernism. As in most great interiors, however, a sense of the owners' personality soon begins to reveal itself. The unconventional aesthetic of the Noailles becomes apparent as one climbs the stairs. Works by Van Dyck, Goya, Burne-Jones, and Juan Gris hang side by side. At the top, the first glimpse of Frank's hand comes into view. Over a great Riesener commode hangs a Picasso still life, suspended by coarse ropes used as though they were the silk cords one would expect. Flanking the commode stand a pair of crude wooden columns, bulging with a rather exaggerated entasis and sitting directly on the floor without any base. On top of the columns rest a pair of identical casts made by Frank of a portrait bust by Houdon. (Albert Hadley has another cast of this Houdon bust as a reminder of Frank and a tribute to his genius.) It is clearly a bit of a tease to place identical casts on top of rough wooden columns. Frank's skill at playing around on a grand scale without slipping into pomposity was one of his most distinctive qualities, and stepping into the Noailles's drawing room, one comes in direct contact with his subtle talent.

This wonderful room is now quite altered from its original state. In its very first period, Frank's scheme consisted of eliminating all moldings from the space and covering the walls with large squares of parchment. The doors, four pairs of them, were sheathed in bronze, as were their simple, flat frames. Large upholstered pieces with overscaled curved arms sat around in a U shape in front of the fireplace. The angles of placement were not strictly squared off, giving the arrangement a pleasingly loose quality, a quality lacking, I might add, in many highly stylized modern rooms both then and now. A few years later the curvy furniture was replaced with much boxier designs, equally bulky but squarer. The arrangement, however, remained both easy and loose. The materials Frank used were plain and light, while the carpet was flat and patternless. The curtains were equally severe. Frank made for the room a number of U-shaped tables of sizes varying from small to very large. They were finished in a variety of his fine marquetry. Low screens stood behind the central sofa and around the grand piano. The fireplace surround was (and is) composed of squares of mica laid up like bricks.

The walls, originally bare, are now covered by paintings; works by Bérard, Dali, and Balthus, to name a few of the artists,

This late work, done in the Argentine, contains the sculptural, plastic forms that were such a great influence on Frances Elkins and Michael Taylor.

hang from chains suspended from a flat picture molding. The hanging of these pictures on walls that Frank thought should be left bare caused him to quarrel with the Noailles. Their uninhibited tampering with his creation was certainly radical. Pictures, books, and objects of all sorts crowd surfaces that were intended to be pristine. Baggy slipcovers with the hint of loving hands render Frank's mammoth upholstery even more inviting, if somewhat less under control. The true strength of the room, a combination of Frank's genius and the intellectual taste of the Noailles, has enabled it to survive through the years. The room is not a set piece, untouched by time. Instead, it represents the rarest qualities of all: great design plus the intensely fascinating evidence of a life of refinement and taste taking place within an atmosphere of beautiful decoration. All that is missing in the reconstructions of period rooms is present in this great twentieth-century document of interior decoration, collecting, and the ephemeral atmosphere of how people of great style live in their surroundings.

What *is* missing in the Noailles rooms after sixty years is the great purity that is visible in the photographs from the thirties. Unlike many decorated rooms in general and most contemporary ones in particular, this loss does not devastate them. Frank's designs possessed a strength that was able to withstand all kinds of interference, and now, after all these years, his pupils (and there are many) are still learning from him. Today, as I finished writing this, I walked across the Place Vendôme to the shop he designed for the perfumer Guerlain in order to buy some of my favorite geranium soap. There again, Frank, in his typical way, used one material as thought it were another. The tiny corner space, paneled in travertine and furnished with console tables of the same stone, is still as chic and severe as ever. The alternating panels and arches still make their unmistakably clear reference to the classical past. The Giacometti plaster shell chandelier still does its job better than many (and maybe most) of its modern-day counterparts. The message of timeless elegance couldn't be clearer or more enduring.

One's respect for Frank's achievement can only increase with the thought of how heartbreakingly brief his career was— just a little over ten years. In 1941 he committed suicide in New York. He had fled Nazism and the war. He had found work in

South America and the United States. His apartment for Templeton Crocker in San Francisco was another legend in the history of decorating. But he couldn't go on. His genius, however, and his creations are an unforgettable legacy.

Syrie Maugham

WENDOLINE MAUD SYRIE BARNARDO WAS born on July 10, 1879, in London, in the large Victorian house of her parents. Her father, a doctor and a minister, was the founder of the Barnardo Homes for Boys and Girls and, as such, he became famous in his time. Her mother, also called Syrie, lived to be ninety-six and, like her daughter, was a bit of a character, known for her uneven temper. But the Barnardos were famous and their favorite child, Queenie, as she was called, grew up being adored and spoiled. Syrie was married briefly to Henry Wellcome, a friend of her father's, who was twenty-six years older than she. They had a son together. The marriage was unhappy and came to an end in 1916 after a six-year separation; the son was never normal and never talked about.

Syrie met Somerset Maugham in 1913 and pursued him

When Mr. and Mrs. Harrison Williams owned this house in Palm Beach, they hired Syrie Maugham, who gave it the look of her early period. It shows the influence of Jean-Michel Frank, which she mixed in with her own softer, more complicated style.

until their marriage in 1917 in New Jersey, where they honeymooned on the seashore in a house belonging to the Doubledays. Their stormy marriage has been written about in many places and it only lasted until 1929. Syrie loved the fact that Maugham was famous and was undeterred by his relationships with men. Their life together was not happy, though. The marriage produced one child, Liza, whom Syrie idolized all of her life.

Syrie's career began in the early twenties when she opened a shop in London, a practice that was common in those days among women wanting to go into business. In a famous quotation of Elsie Mendl's, when Syrie had asked Elsie if she could go into business with her, Elsie replied no, that she was much too late. The decorating business was already too full. But Syrie Maugham's shop was enough of a success for her to continue, and soon she began to decorate, primarily for herself at first, in a glamorous and fresh way that caught the attention of magazine editors and socialites and therefore of the public as well. In the late twenties she decorated two houses for herself and Somerset Maugham, although by then they were spending a great deal of time apart. The first of these houses was in the French seaside resort of Le Touquet. The second was her legendary house in the King's Road in Chelsea, in London, which had at the back, in Glebe Place, a smaller house, which she connected by a beautiful hallway.

The house in Le Touquet, with its white fur rugs and large upholstered furniture covered in bold stripes and rough-textured damask and Tudor-style tables that had been lightened in the popular limed-oak finish of the time, was casual, soft, and comfortable, very much a weekend place. With its blend of contemporary sleekness and old-fashioned rusticity, it differed from the

more sumptuous approach that quickly took over in her decorating. The pale tonality associated with Syrie was already evident, though, and so was the quality of softness combined with
simple, contemporary lines.

The house in the King's Road had even more elements that
will always be identified with Syrie. The most memorable aspect
of that house, however, apart from her frequent parties and her
superb food, was the enormous drawing room that she decorated
in many shades of white. There had been earlier waves of white
in decorating that caused considerable comment and excitement.
Philip Webb and Charles Rennie Mackintosh realized its poten-
tial. Elsie de Wolfe, too, used a lot of white paint. But Syrie's
room was bolder than most of its predecessors. It was a room
that instantly became famous. It drew an incredible amount of
attention to her career, which was just beginning, after all, although she was at the time in her late forties. The all-white
drawing room had sofas slipcovered in satin, a huge mirrored
screen composed of about thirty narrow panels of mirror edged
in silver-leafed metal, a white geometric carpet by the designer
Marion Dorn, white wooden tables in the style of Jean-Michel
Frank, lampshades mysteriously described as being made of
white velvet, a thought that's hard to deal with in this day and
age, and all white flowers. Given the later style that we associate
with Syrie Maugham, the white room in the King's Road house
was very severe. No other room that she decorated was quite
as strictly modernistic and probably no other room was as famous. At exactly the same time, the English architect Oliver Hill
and the French decorator Jean-Michel Frank were working in a
parallel idiom. Their work was more architectural and more
doctrinaire than Syrie's, but there are remarkable similarities.

Syrie Maugham's last drawing room in London was
stripped of its architectural
details and filled with the
gamut of her trademarks,
from English and French
furniture to plaster palm
trees and a Giacometti lamp.
The Swedish commode ended
up in the hall of the Duke
and Duchess of Windsor.

The screen that hid Syrie's piano was very like one that Jean-Michel Frank placed around the piano in the Paris drawing room of Marie-Laure de Noailles. I always wonder if Syrie hadn't already met Frank. She certainly followed his career through his shops in Paris during the thirties.

The rest of the house in the King's Road exhibited the more voluptuous, rococo, and feminine side of Syrie's taste, which was in fact the side that asserted itself over and over again throughout her career. The materials and elements that she continued to use for the next twenty years are interesting in that they provide a look at what she introduced in decorating and what became identified with her style, as well as what influenced the styles of other decorators. Dining chairs were frequently covered in white leather. White porcelain, particularly porcelain birds, appeared in her rooms over and over again. White porcelain-handled knives were a trademark. Her mixture of English and French furniture was thoroughgoing. She particularly liked graceful curves: Louis XV furniture in all of its phases, authentic and inauthentic. She was not in the least daunted by reproductions. Fringes were used to trim curtains, furniture, and pillows, in an enormously luxurious and sometimes overstated way. Moss fringe lined the seams of overstuffed furniture; great long fringes swirled around in scrolled patterns on valances and down the fronts of curtains. The color tones that she used, because in fact she worked with color a lot—it was *not* just the all-white room that interested her—were beautiful, delicate, and soft. She used sapphire blue with whites, often piping blue furniture with white. The sitting room in her later country house, which took the place of Le Touquet, had pink walls, ivory curtains, and apple-green and red furniture, all combined with antique needlework

carpets. She loved rock crystal and mirrors, often covering bathroom walls and screens and furniture itself with mirrors, as other people were doing at the time; however, she did it in a particularly rich way that was refined rather than appearing like something out of the ladies' room in a nightclub. She was devoted to satin and shiny surfaces and swirls of plasterwork, with rococo scrolls as well as plant forms and palm fronds. She adored bamboo, which appeared again and again in tables and chairs and architectural details. The flowers in her rooms were always considered a great element of the design and she was an early client of Constance Spry, the brilliant London florist. The plasterwork that she loved so much was sometimes designed by Oliver Messel, the great scenic designer. It's interesting that Syrie, with her love of theatrical and indeed almost ephemeral rooms filled with delicate colors and furniture of no serious value, should be closely involved with a man whose chief occupation was in theatre design. She used white rugs throughout her career, in wool and sheepskin. In addition, she loved faded antique carpets. Her furniture was said by John Fowler to be the best-made upholstery in London. When she slipcovered it, she liked the slipcovers to have a sort of dowdy, homemade look. When she was in New York living at the Dakota during World War II, she had a maid named Doris who sewed slipcovers in the rather offhand, homemade way that appealed to Syrie, who thought American upholsterers made them look too tailored and too stiff. Her rooms always combined a mixture of old and new. There was never any atmosphere of a period room being recreated nor, after the all-white room in the late twenties, was there ever a room that appeared to be frankly all new and modern. Although she hated Victorian furniture and was very vocal on the subject, she was fond of tufting and she worked with many Victorian furniture shapes, revising them, simplifying them, and bringing them into the present in forms that we still recognize today. Many of these pieces still carry her name. Her fully upholstered and fringed sleigh bed is familiar to all sophisticated upholsterers. She would put little tufts on anything that she fancied would be improved by this rather soft detail. A finish that she was famous for was crackled paint, and in her workshops she had two or three people who were known to be particularly skilled at putting a craquelure on any wooden surface. Her whites were known to have an old quality to them; they weren't the starchy, bright whites that we are so used to now. She was famous for her screens and she made them out of lacquer, mirrors, photomontages, and materials of all sorts. She used shells frequently; made of plaster or wood, they would appear in all kinds of forms in her furniture. Large, exaggerated dolphin console tables were used in hallways and dining rooms again and again. She was known at the time to like Regency furniture when other people considered it not serious enough to be valued. She, however, always loved it. Her mirrorwork extended often to fireplace surrounds in many designs, another element of the twenties and thirties which she particularly championed.

What is fascinating and impressive about the work of Syrie Maugham is that she worked with this long, rambling list of favorite things throughout the twenty-five years of her career without ever abandoning them or giving in to momentary changes of heart. She was always loyal to her first loves, and she mixed them in a way that always bore her signature but continued to have a lively originality, infusing her rooms with a graceful, rather delicate beauty that made them romantic and enticing. They had none of the practical, workaday quality that gives some decorating an obvious, safe appeal. Her work had an extravagant quality about it, without seeming frightfully rich or ostentatious. Still, her rooms appealed to a sense of extravagance. The Syrie Maugham style was never monumental or grand in an architectural way, and it was not at home in great English country houses.

Like so many decorators who became legendary, Syrie had, to her great credit, a long list of famous clients, who were themselves legends. The very fact that they hired her went a long way toward creating her fame. In the thirties she was known

Gertrude Lawrence's bed, called a Syrie Maugham bed after the decorator, was combined with a Marion Dorn carpet, a Venetian chair, and a night table all used repeatedly by Syrie.

to be a friend of the Prince of Wales and Mrs. Simpson, and although it is not known exactly how much work she did for them, she did help them with the rooms at Fort Belvedere, the Prince's Gothic weekend villa near London. If one looks at the later houses of the Duke and Duchess of Windsor, houses that were always worked on by Jansen in Paris, there are still lingering traces of Syrie Maugham's taste, a memory of her fondness for a certain kind of French furniture, delicate color schemes, lots of soft upholstery details that are clearly hers and no one else's. She also did an enormous amount of work in America for people whose personal style was always in the spotlight. In fact, her influence in the United States was far more enduring than in England. The comparative simplicity of the new architecture surely accounts for this phenomenon. The great English traditions of decorating simply were too much at odds with her chic, iconoclastic style.

Mrs. Harrison Williams was one of those stylish society clients who was thought to be richer and more beautiful than anybody else around. Syrie Maugham created for her, both in New York and in Palm Beach, rooms typical of her style. Though it does not sound like an important element of design, they were particularly memorable for their fabulous flowers, which Mrs. Williams's greenhouses would produce all year round.

Babs Simpson, another member of the world of rarefied taste and a longtime Condé Nast editor, whose apartment Syrie decorated in the forties, remembers Syrie as being generous and devoted to her clients. Full of a wicked wit, she could be very funny, although she was also known to be irascible and irritable and sharp-tongued. Still, she was a source of great amusement to the people for whom she worked. She worked on the beautiful houses of Mr. and Mrs. Woolcott Blair, who lived in Chicago, Palm Beach, and Long Island. Syrie's refined and rather offbeat style appealed very much to Mrs. Blair, whose own style was unequaled and who worked over the years with David Adler and Frances Elkins and Ruby Ross Wood as well. Syrie's letters to Mrs. Blair, which still exist, are full of pleas for forgiveness with regard to lampshades that cost too much or furniture from London that was late or, again, was too extravagantly priced. She was famous for her high prices and for certain questionable practices—copying chairs and calling them old, for example. She even had a dreadful run-in with the IRS over her records. It was said that the Williamses in Palm Beach fell out with Syrie because some of the furniture she sold them never appeared in the house but showed up for sale in her new Palm Beach shop. The stories surrounding her career are full of examples of a rather bold and fearless ability to take advantage of her clients. Of course she landed in hot water some of the time.

She worked on the beautiful David Adler house in California belonging to Mrs. Tobin Clark. It is described in most books on decorating as marking a high point in the design of the thirties, and its white bedroom with painted and fringed furniture and wall panels decorated in green scrolls is reproduced in dozens of books. It is a room that inspired many followers. Later on, in the forties, she worked both for Mr. and Mrs. Paul Mellon and for Mr. and Mrs. William Paley. When I first saw the Paleys' drawing room in Long Island, it still bore the marks of Syrie's hand, with stenciled, damask-patterned canvas on the walls, masses of curved, tufted sofas and chairs, and a faded color scheme of pale aquamarine, many shades of white, and a rich, dark claret red as an accent. The carpet was plain, solid green wool velvet. The room had the light, blurred color quality that I think must have been common in Syrie's rooms, with a hazy mood created by pale tones and yards of satin and velvet, resulting in an atmosphere of terrific glamour. The Paleys' drawing room was distinguished by being filled with paintings by Cézanne, Rousseau, Toulouse-Lautrec, and Matisse. The Mellons' rooms with their unsurpassed pictures, still reflect the Syrie Maugham dislike of stuffy richness.

Syrie's own rooms, and many of the rooms she decorated for her clients, are noteworthy for having very little art on the walls. This was a point of view shared by Jean-Michel Frank, I might point out, who always discouraged his clients from hanging pictures. Syrie was really not concerned with a lot of what we think of nowadays as being of great importance in decorating. She was not interested in serious, important furniture. When she said, "Cut it down and paint it white," she was not referring to an Adam cabinet or a William Kent settee. Nor did she have a great interest in historical accuracy as far as architectural details were concerned. She was devoted in an unabashed way to prettiness and luxury and creating surroundings of tremendous comfort and romantic extravagance that made it clear that her rooms were meant for people of special privilege. They were not rooms concerned with practical day-to-day problems of housekeeping and economy. Her use of white was almost a belligerent act, after all. Their carefree quality gave her rooms a kind of snobbish appeal that was on the cutting edge of her designs throughout her career. She was not interested in creations that were applicable to everyday circumstances; one could never imagine her teaching the fundamentals of decorating to others. There was a free-handed, throw-caution-to-the-winds spirit that, combined with her great ability to create soft, romantic beauty, has made her an unforgettable idol of people who have wanted to decorate and it gave to her rooms an unmistakable quality that to this day is always recognizable and continues to be emulated by people seeking a solution to the mundane problems of decorating. Every decorator I have ever known with any awareness of the past has felt some kind of admiration for the Syrie Maugham style. From Dorothy Draper to Albert Hadley and Michael Taylor, there is a continuous line of influence based on her innovative talent. The endurance of her designs is proof of her originality and her appeal.

Billy Baldwin

IT COULD BE SAID OF BILLY BALDWIN THAT he was the most beloved interior decorator of his time. In fact, given the sharp-tongued tendencies of the design world, he might go down in history as the most popular decorator there ever was. It is not difficult to explain this. He was, to use his favorite word, the most attractive person anyone could imagine. Armed with a keenly intelligent mind, a delicious gift for conversation which never ignored the importance of facts, and perfect manners, which kept a rein on his always amusing stories, he was the best possible companion. Unlike many of the chic and famous, he never conveyed that threat of boredom lying just below the surface. He was generous and adorable. His taste, which, after all, was central to his career as a decorator, was full of paradoxes. He loved luxury, but he abhorred conspicuous richness. His aim was to be stylish at all

Cole Porter's Waldorf Tower library was a remarkable, trendsetting room for the next thirty years or so. It proves that modern design can embrace the objects of the past without corrupting its own philosophy.

times, but trendy vulgarity could not have been more remote from his work. He had the instincts of a modernist, but the framework within which he worked was classical and traditional.

In his autobiography, a not altogether successful memoir dictated shortly before his death, he laid out pretty clearly the things in life that meant most to him. Good breeding was a crucial element in the makeup of any really worthwhile person. Because he was unpretentious himself, his opinions about the status of others did not seem particularly harsh, but people with common or vulgar ways never got very far with Billy. You could say he had high standards, in the broadest sense. He grew up in a family that noticed the material side of life and cared about its own impression on the world. Not many figures in history have described their father's wardrobe as being a threat to the family's financial stability; Billy's book, however, is full of comments about his father's sartorial extravagance (a reminder never to discuss one's tailor's bills in front of the children). In life, Billy would never have spoken of his parents in such a way. His code of behavior would not have permitted it. It is illuminating, though, to learn that the paternal example had a lot to do with clothes. Billy's own wardrobe was immaculate and handsome. Only once did I ever see him dressed in a way that was a little out of hand. He was wearing a strange navy-blue overcoat that had been designed for him by Hardy Amies. With it, he was carrying a leather envelope, not really a briefcase, made of red hide the color of a royal dispatch box. Usually he was dressed in a perfect Anglo-American way, with a trace of the Duke of Windsor, who was, after all, part of Billy's world. Wallis (the Duchess of Windsor) was born in Baltimore, and so was Billy. The old-fashioned hunt country ways of that part of the world were both an influence and an ideal to the very elegant man who left there in his thirties (he was born in 1903), after having worked in the decorating business in Baltimore, for a career in New York. He began that career as an assistant to Ruby Ross Wood, a legendary figure in the design world, who had come to New York from Georgia and therefore shared Billy's reverence for Southern manners; you understand that Baltimoreans consider themselves Southern. Mrs. Wood, as Billy always referred to her, was married to a fox-hunting man and lived the kind of life Billy admired. So, from the moment he arrived in New York in 1935 until Mrs. Wood's death in 1950, Billy worked in close association with a mentor of renown who seems to have been the most sympathetic of employers. She also possessed the gift of really *great* taste. Without ever undergoing any wrenching changes, his style proceeded to develop in an uninterrupted flow.

More than anything else, the force that shaped Billy's life and career was his love of a kind of stylish glamour tempered by a concern with being correct. When it came to decorating, the correctness that he imposed on all of his rooms resulted primarily from his love of tradition along with his distaste for all ostentation. To Billy, many of the elements of decoration that are so popular now were hopelessly excessive and even vulgar. His love of cotton materials is well known. The silks that he used in city rooms were always understated and retiring, resembling cotton some of the time. He often preferred paper lampshades to silk ones. When he wanted to be rich, he sometimes used velvet, particularly a silk velvet from France with a pattern of little squares. If his curtains were topped with valances, the valances were tailored and plain. Although he used English furniture frequently, the English house was not an inspiration to

him. A version of Parisian chic was much more up his alley, and long before anyone in New York talked about Madeleine Castaing, Billy was tearing around from client to client using her paisley carpets, her twisted rope stools and chairs, and completely getting her point. Historic styles weren't of great concern to him, either. What *was* of interest was the style of the times. His rooms were not trendy; they were, however, rooms for people of fashion and they were very much up to date. As an admirer once said of him, he knew how a beautiful, chic woman should live. He understood all the facets of housekeeping, and the people he worked for, more than with most decorators, fitted his concept of the ideal. For Billy, being in fashion was terribly important. Two of his greatest friends throughout his life, who would have enormous influence on him, were themselves people of great personal style, who were involved professionally in the world of fashion and design. One of them was Pauline Potter, who later became the Baronne de Rothschild. Born in Baltimore like Billy, from her earliest years she showed incredible interest and originality in her approach to fashion. She came to New York to work for Hattie Carnegie and immediately became known for the unique look of her apartment, as well as the individuality of her clothes. She designed and she decorated. Everything she touched had great flair. The single most important characteristic of her early decorating style was her fondness for rooms that were nearly empty, a few pieces of very good furniture arranged not for large crowds but to show off the quality of the pieces themselves and to create an atmosphere, if not of deep cozy comfort, at least of great visual beauty with a bit of a shocking effect as well. Her rooms in her French homes,

Mrs. Clive Runnells's Hobe Sound living room, with its Syrie Maugham sofa, Jean-Michel Frank table, and Frances Elkins color scheme, reflected three of Billy's perennial influences.

in Paris and at Mouton, were, as everyone knows, seminal, trend-setting exercises in exotic, luxurious originality.

Another friend and mentor for the greater part of Billy's adult life was Van Day Truex. Van was born in Kansas in 1904, a year after Billy's birth, and he came to New York, where he attended the Parsons School of Design. Later he studied in Paris, where there was a famous branch of the Parsons School. He eventually became the head of the school's Paris branch. Van's style was more modern than Billy's, more progressive in its outlook. Through Van, Billy was in touch with current design trends, especially those in Europe and particularly those in Paris. That fact had a huge influence on how Billy viewed the modern world of decorating. Van was a great admirer of Jean-Michel Frank and passed that admiration on to Billy. One of the trademarks of Van's style was the woven straw Jean-Michel Frank chair, which became a staple in Billy's decoration of both summer and winter rooms. Straw, rattan, and bamboo appeared constantly in his schemes, always lightening the effect of his rooms. Van and Pauline Potter were legendary figures from the point of view of how they dressed, how they decorated, and how they entertained. The food, the table settings, the flowers, the lighting, the clothes they wore: it was this thorough view of what people do in the beautiful rooms that are decorated for them—how they look in them and how they entertain in them—that meant so much to Billy and was central to his way of decorating for his clients. His rooms were created for people of great style who were supposed to look good in them. To be totally comfortable in these surroundings was equally important. Billy's work was entirely appropriate for the people who commissioned it.

The great clients whose names come to mind immediately

The Paleys' Fifth Avenue library possessed grand aspects of Parisian decoration, from Louis XV and XVI to Matisse. The bookcases with Roman busts peering down at you remind one of Charles de Beistegui.

and whose work done by Billy is so memorable were, like Van and Pauline Potter, also people of tremendous personal style, real glamour, and sometimes even beauty. For years, Billy did a number of houses and apartments in New York, in London, outside of London, and in Portugal for Mrs. Gilbert Miller, the famous Kitty Miller, who was eternally best dressed, very rich, a great, great hostess, and who conducted all of this busy, stylish life in rooms created for her by Billy Baldwin. Her apartment at 550 Park Avenue was enormous and pale and immaculate, exuding that instant sense of fantastic housekeeping which could be perceived the minute you stepped through the door. The big drawing room, which was really two rooms that had been thrown together by Billy, was renowned for the Goya portrait of the little boy in the red suit, which hung on the wall between the windows opposite the fireplace. For half of every year it hung at the Met. Mrs. Miller's father, Jules Bache, had left it jointly to her and to the museum. As she grew older, it became annually more and more difficult for the Met to get the painting back. No wonder! The furniture was French and light in scale, covered in unobtrusive silks in soft tones. The curtains, equally light, were made of striped silk and, rather than having elaborate trims and valances, they were made in the simplest possible way, trimmed with a self-stripe and hung from a very plain top molding covered in the same material as the curtains themselves. The atmosphere of luxurious pallor that existed in this room was also present in Mrs. Miller's large drawing room on Hill Street, in London. In many ways, these rooms showed the influence of Syrie Maugham on Billy's work. He always said that she was one of his idols. The house in Portugal that Billy decorated for the Millers in the sixties was loaded with the straw furniture and Porthault printed cotton and white plaster lamps that by then were a trademark of his style. Some of this look dated from the thirties, when he first arrived in New York, and it calls to mind Frances Elkins, another huge influence on Billy. A characteristic of Billy's work is the fact that he never abandoned the trademarks that he loved so much; he did not allow them, on the other hand, to become dull-looking and ossified.

Another of the grand clients important to Billy for a long period of time was Mrs. Clive Runnells, whose houses in Lake

Forest, Illinois, and Hobe Sound, Florida, he worked on for over twenty years. Mrs. Runnells was another of the chic ladies who typified Billy's ideals in decorating, in fashion—and in society for that matter. The house in Lake Forest was unlike most of Billy's houses. Filled with English antiques, it nevertheless had the light, immaculate, rather new look that Billy favored. He was never one for old, worn-out rooms. The drawing-room colors were crisp and fresh, confined to shades of green and white and dominated by a large-scale pattern, with a Cogolin carpet from France, one of those very expensive and rather unobtrusive handmade carpets that Billy loved—they always took nine months or a year to make, and because they were slow to be delivered, very expensive, and rather understated, you can imagine that they were not popular with many decorators. They were *exactly* what Billy liked. Mrs. Runnells's house in Hobe Sound was all blue and white, with lots of white lacquer, navy-blue upholstery piped in white, white rugs, and red Chinese and Japanese lacquer accessories. Strictly symmetrical in a way that Billy often preferred to arrange large rooms, and with a slightly thirties look to the upholstery, the room had the sleek, well-organized appearance that infused all of his work. One of the most famous people he worked for was Cole Porter, and one of the most celebrated jobs he ever did was the composer's Waldorf Tower apartment. Decorated in the fifties, its atmosphere was one of spare, luxurious, French refinement with no sense of clutter or overpowering overstuffedness. In fact it was decidedly sparse-looking. The drawing room had beautiful antique parquet and groups of rather delicate French furniture arranged on antique carpets that created "islands" on the parquet floor. The walls were hung with eighteenth-century Chinese export wallpaper. The library, which was the most memorable room in the apartment, had shiny tortoiseshell lacquered leather walls. All around them were brass bookshelves in a Directoire design that were filled with Cole Porter's everyday collection of books, not just those in fancy bindings. The furniture in the room was covered in beiges or in tan leather. The carpet was off-white. The furniture consisted of polished wood pieces, in Louis XV and Louis XVI styles. The whole atmosphere of the room was very tawny and calm. This library was one of those great decorating feats that captured the imagination of everybody who saw it. It was widely copied in every possible respect.

At the same time that Billy was doing this legendary apartment, he was given another interesting hotel commission, the St. Regis apartment for Mr. and Mrs. William Paley. Like Mrs. Miller and Mrs. Runnells, Babe Paley was a paragon of best-dressed glamour, as well as a great beauty. The Paley style was a source of awe to many who encountered it. The drawing room in the St. Regis apartment, with its Beaux-Arts bronze doré and marble mantel and high ceilings, was hung in shirred paisley with a soft brown background. The resulting effect of this shirred material was rather stuffy, unlike his more characteristic crisp, hard-edged look. But he dealt with it in a light-handed way that prevented the stuffiness from becoming overwhelming. The furniture was covered in light-colored materials or in the paisley of the walls. On the floor there was a beautiful needlepoint carpet with blackamoors' heads woven into the squares in its pattern. Overhead hung a nineteenth-century Venetian chandelier containing a pair of struggling blackamoors and a clock of chinoiserie Brighton Pavilion confusion. The upholstered furniture in the room had the lines, if not the finished details, of the Second

Kitty Miller's outdoor terrace in Mallorca was organized along strictly symmetrical lines. Plaster lamps from the thirties marry perfectly with the Saarinen tables from the fifties.

Empire, a style that Billy used sparingly at a time when others in America were not using it at all. He always modified it and translated it into a cleaner design, but he was careful to retain the proportions of the original frames, the rope-twisted stools, and so on, that are so much a part of this now popular period of decoration. The room was repeated, years later, when the Paleys moved from the St. Regis to Fifth Avenue, and existed until recently with its chinoiserie chandelier and tented walls. The needlepoint carpet, which disappeared long ago, was replaced by a copy in modern needlepoint, and the French furniture was added to, so that the room became grander than Billy's original concept. But the same great style remained. Once again, a decorator of modern times doing a room in this style would be tempted to use a lot of velvet and fringe and heavy cording, but Billy, typically, used cotton instead. Only rich passementerie tiebacks revealed any love of fancy trimmings.

Another room of Billy's that was a landmark in decorating, not only because it was very bold and photographable, but also because it belonged to a woman of overwhelming style, was the drawing room on Park Avenue that he did for Diana Vreeland. It was, as she so often said, meant to look like a garden, but a garden in hell. The material he used in both the drawing room and the bedroom (although in different colorways) was the large, overscale pattern of leaves and branches printed in France, taken from the designs of Indian prints and Indian embroidery and so popular with Madeleine Castaing, a decorator who greatly influenced Billy's decorating style. Billy in fact found a slightly varied version of this tree of life printed in Spain, and it was an exclusive with him, so to speak. This room managed to have a clean look because of the way Billy approached the design of the banquettes and the upholstered furniture and because of the orderly way in which the clutter was arranged. It was, in fact, wildly cluttered, with collections everywhere of horn, tortoise-shell, porcelain, and wooden objects. The table tops were so full that there was no place for a drink. But it was all organized in a program of extreme neatness and the room, in spite of all its exotica, had that atmosphere of tidiness that was a trademark of Billy's decorating.

Later in his career he decorated a large, Georgian-style house in Washington for Mr. and Mrs. William McCormick Blair. Deeda Blair is another one of Billy's ideal ladies whose clothes, food, and flowers are all part of the aura of the complete creature of fashion that he so admired. The house in Washington, more than most houses, has a coherent, all-over effect that Billy achieved with Mrs. Blair by imposing on it a strict rule of design, color, and style. Most of the furniture throughout the house is Louis XVI, with lesser touches of Louis XV thrown in. The color scheme, always based on off-whites, has as its main accents greens and browns or green and pale blues. The patterns used are clear and sharply defined. There is a prevailing sharpness of line that lends to every room a sparkling clarity that feels continuously new and clean. Billy, after all, used geometrics before anyone else. The Blair house was, and is, a tour de force of cool freshness. At the same time, it contains the promise of luxury that made so many of Billy's houses deliciously inviting.

The most luxurious of all houses, with the most mysteriously understated subtlety imaginable, are those belonging to Mrs. Paul Mellon, for whom Billy worked as well and whom he admired with the same fervor as do all those who are familiar with her genius. Perhaps no ideal was ever as completely realized for Billy as the example of Mrs. Mellon. Despite his love of uncluttered understatement, Billy's real passion was for that rare individual whose consuming interest in living and whose brilliant taste combined to produce a house, a garden, a collection, and a wardrobe perfectly suited to a subtle and unostentatious daily life of original and personal refinement. It was a very romantic notion, but he never gave it up.

Dorothy Draper

THE PERSONAL SAGAS OF DECORATORS ARE often interesting, revealing as they do the process by which these individuals turn themselves into personalities capable of dominating large areas of other people's private lives, as well as their preoccupation with society: who's who, the world of grand hostesses, and all the talk about the Duchess of Windsor—frequent obsessions in the world of decorators. The women who laid the foundation of the decorating trade exemplified the pre-World War II mold of ladylike behavior, excepting the fact that they were ambitious and bold. The odium of publicity held by their clients and their clients' mothers, who felt one's name should appear in the newspapers only when one was born, married, and finally died, never pricked the conscience of those who took up decorating. To be correct without sacrificing their chic lent credence to their business

Dorothy Draper's mischievous urge to shock led her to combine three strong shades of green with tomato red. That she addressed herself to ordinary apartments for her enormous public is apparent from the simple architecture of this room with its confusion of beams.

claims. If Elsie de Wolfe and her successors were not exactly the daughters of dukes and grandees, they were certainly very much a part of the social world whose members made up their clientele. It was critical to their careers to maintain this connection with society; it legitimized their positions as arbiters of taste. Although Lady Bracknell in *The Importance of Being Earnest* held that lawyers were not seen in society, the same could not be said of interior decorators, in spite of complaints from their betters.

Dorothy Draper, who went into business over sixty-five years ago (about the same time Eleanor McMillen was opening her firm) possessed all the attributes common to her contemporaries in the decorating field. She was full of self-confidence and comfortable in her views about the taste of the time, which she considered greatly in need of new stimulation. Other decorators shared this opinion, yet they all chose to represent themselves as unique visionaries soldiering on in their solitary way. One can't imagine Elsie or Syrie saying, "Then *we* did this or *we* did that." The first person singular was their pronoun, and it was Dorothy Draper's too. Furthermore, her husband, a doctor, did not make enough money to suit her, providing her with a further incentive to turn to a career of her own. But Dorothy Draper differed from her competitors in one very significant way: they blended in with the world of the rich and stylish— she had been born into it. So had her husband. Her innate feeling of superiority played an active role in making Dorothy Draper, within twenty years, the most famous name in American decorating.

She was born in 1889. Her parents, Mr. and Mrs. Paul Tuckerman of Tuxedo Park, were part of an American elite who considered themselves members of a continuously distinguished lineage reaching back to the earliest days of our colonial history. They were rich, but not as rich as the nouveaux riches, doubtless a point of honor in their book. Their daughter, whom they called Star (if you can believe it), grew up to be a beautiful girl who hated school and, luckily for her, didn't have to suffer through much of it. Two years at Brearley are all that appear on the records. At the age of twenty-three, she married Dr. George Draper, whom she had known since her debutante year and who was a man of charm, intelligence, and culture. They had three children—two girls and a boy. Like her cousin, Sister Parish (twenty years her junior), whose first house in New Jersey was so charming that it immediately led others to seek her advice, Dorothy's early decorating projects as a young wife were met with such enthusiasm that one Draper house was sold lock, stock, and barrel, enabling the astonished housewife to set out all over again and create a second adorable house. These were the years of the First World War, when Dan Draper (as he was called) was posted to Washington. After the war the Drapers returned to New York and to a brief year of boredom and dissatisfaction for Dorothy. Part of her unhappiness was caused by her jealousy of the more cerebral women of the Draper family, especially Dan Draper's younger sister, Ruth, the brilliant monologuist whose career was earning her lots of praise and lots of money in America and England. But the real root of Dorothy's impatience with her life derived from those qualities which made her so perfectly suited to the business career in her future. She was neither cozy nor domestic. Being a mother was of little interest to her, and she was determined to be recognized on her own. As Eleanor Roosevelt (Franklin had gone to Groton with Dan

Draper) said of her many years later, she was like a "little boy who is showing off and says, 'See what I can do?'" Having remodeled a couple of houses in Washington and one in New York, all before she was thirty-five, Dorothy Draper decided, in 1925, to open a business called the Architectural Clearing House, which matched the appropriate architect to various projects in her new field of interest. Then, through a family friend, she got what was a seminal commission, the decoration of the lobby of the new Carlyle Hotel. Significantly, her family connections were a factor in this career turning point. The Tuxedo Park upbringing that distinguished Dorothy Draper from others in her field was an essential part of the personal stamp that gave her so much authority over her customers. She scorned private decoration in favor of public, commercial work, and her customers, the "tiny tycoons" as they were often called (why were they so often short?), were simply not her equals. The private world of Dorothy Draper did not include people who hired her.

The decoration of the Carlyle lobby pointed in the direction her style would follow for the next thirty years: crisply geometric marble floors in black, grey, and white, immaculate white plaster, and lush, tufted furniture with a touch of Belle Époque opulence. Only the antique tapestries from Rose Cumming's shop (still in place sixty years later) fell into the traditional vocabulary of hotel-lobby decoration.

Shortly after the success of the Carlyle, Mrs. Draper's next big opportunity came when the Phipps family real estate concern asked her to come up with a plan to make a block of Sutton Place tenement flats more attractive. Her bold solution was really very simple. Everyone loved the scheme of black brick with starchily white trim and brilliantly colored front doors, each one

Mrs. and Mrs. Albert Lasker's Beekman Place townhouse was decorated throughout with white as the basic color. Strict symmetry and hard edges counteracted the blurry softness. The real impact was the collection of twentieth-century French paintings.

different. The face lift was a success, both critically for Dorothy Draper and financially for the owners. But as her career was taking off, her marriage was coming to a halt. In 1929, Dr. Draper announced that he was leaving her. From that moment on, there would be very little conflict in her life; her career dominated everything and, in spite of the Depression, it accelerated with remarkable speed. The name of her firm was promptly changed to Dorothy Draper. Her grand relations, who had thought her brazen when she first went into business, must have been astonished by the "DD" (as she came to be called) and the explosion of newspaper and magazine coverage that followed her from one job to another. Her evolving style was equally brazen.

The 1930s began for Dorothy Draper's newly christened company with the job of decorating the recently built River Club. It was another huge success. By the end of the decade she was writing a column for the Hearst papers and working on a book, all from her new apartment at the Hampshire House, the Central Park South monument to her fully evolved style that, more than any other job, established her as the leading design personality in the country.

During the twenties and thirties numerous designers here and abroad experimented with a revival of baroque and rococo decorative arts. Some, like Jean-Michel Frank, were modernist and surreal in their approach. Others, like Rex Whistler, were more historical and romantic in their interpretations. Syrie Maugham was inspired by the complete range of architects, designers, and even cinema art directors (or did she influence them?). There were, to be sure, plenty of precedents for the sort of high drama that was so natural to Dorothy Draper. Edwin Lutyens's last great house, Middleton Park, designed in the first half of the 1930s, with its extravagantly patterned black and white marble floors and its Art Deco plaster shells in the principal bathroom, would have thrilled Mrs. Draper. So would the walls that Lutyens painted black throughout his career. When the Hampshire House commission came along in 1937, Dorothy was prepared to present her growing public with a coherent program of decoration that was all hers, regardless of the contributions of others, including Lester Grundy, her indispensable new assistant. (He became, many years later, a senior member of the editorial corps in the New York world of decorating magazines.) The stylish theatricality of her work at the Hampshire House is still visible. At the time of its unveiling, it must have seemed like a Busby Berkeley movie come to life. The strongest impression at first glance is made by the boldly modeled and overscaled plasterwork in the form of leafy applied moldings on the ceilings, and a fantastic version of a Chinese Chippendale overmantel design that covers the entire chimney breast, on the brackets of which stand blanc de chine figures. The door surrounds and the fireplace opening are all made of mirrored glass bolection moldings reminiscent of the work of David Adler. The color scheme is dominated by white, black, and grey. Her memorable floor is composed of huge squares of black and white marble laid in a checkerboard pattern. White plaster busts stand on shapely pedestals that would have suited works by Bernini or Rysbrack. This was a perfect background for people who lived in an era that still possessed tremendous glamour. Nowadays one thinks how much more stylish New York seemed thirty years ago, but fancy what it must have been like *fifty* years ago!

Dorothy Draper's forceful sense of self and her social su-

Mrs. Ben Sonnenberg's Grammercy Park bedroom was entirely decorated in red and green with lots of brass and gilt. The pier mirror now hangs in the library of Governor and Mrs. Abraham Ribicoff.

periority propelled her fearlessly toward the commercial work that established her wide fame. Working for great ladies of fashion would have driven her crazy and she simply didn't do it. The body of private work in her portfolio is very slight. Most memorable of the houses she decorated was the mammoth, rambling Gramercy Park townhouse belonging to Mr. and Mrs. Benjamin Sonnenberg. According to Carleton Varney's biography of Mrs. Draper, she was unkind about Ben, as many people were. He was a public relations man, *the* public relations man, as a matter of fact. He was, moreover, not a part of the social milieu that Mrs. Draper belonged to and held in such high esteem. He had formidable style, though, and the Sonnenberg house was, in the years I knew it, a joy to see. The parties there were huge and extravagant and packed with brain power. The host was superb. His collections of pictures, furniture, and objects covered an unmemorizable range of periods and styles. Furthermore, in my opinion, Dorothy Draper's hand never looked better, another example of the correctness of the adage that a designer does his best work for a client who has great style. From the overscaled damask wallpaper in Stanford White's stairwell to the red damask and chintz top-floor salon, with its William Kent bookcase, the Dorothy Draper trademarks reached a peak of warmth and charm and beauty never possible in the lobbies of hotels. The office suite she designed for Ben, full of tufted leather, dark walls, and tartan curtains and pelmets, might have come from an Edwardian shooting lodge in Scotland or perhaps the late Henry McIlhenny's house in Ireland.

Both Mr. Sonnenberg and Mrs. Draper agreed on the effectiveness of dark walls, they parted company, however, on the policy of painting furniture white, a favorite Draper touch. She hated brown, and this antipathy seems to have extended to mahogany. She also belittled collectors of antiques, calling them insecure. In light of the fact that she was so proud of her inherited furniture and portraits, one has the feeling that she was a little too vain about her family. It isn't easy, though, to find people who are modest about their grand ancestors, and Mrs. Draper's were part of her stock in trade—literally.

The climax of her career came about after the Second World War, when she was chosen to redecorate the Greenbrier Hotel in West Virginia. Her work there, with all the reds and greens and corals, the oversized stripes and flowers, the glossy white paint, and the frothy white ornamental plasterwork created such a sensation and has endured for so long that her name is *still*

Her great hotel work marked the peak of Dorothy Draper's career. The baroque, Victorian excesses of San Francisco's Fairmont Hotel were perfectly suited to her style.

linked in everyone's mind with the hotel she did so much to revive. It opened in 1948 and, although it might have seemed like the beginning of an era, it was in fact the end. Mrs. Draper was almost sixty years old and in a few more years she would see fifties trends begin to erode the crisp classicism she had combined with huge scale and bold colors to make a vividly recognizable style. The era of orange and turquoise had begun.

But many of her creations endured for decades to come.

The Camellia House in the Drake Hotel in Chicago (1940), another exercise in cyclopean, baroque plasterwork and over-scale flowers, this time using camellias in place of the trademark cabbage rose, remained untouched for over twenty years. The Roman-inspired restaurant at the Metropolitan Museum (1954) still sports many of her design elements, notably the immense light fixtures; only recently were any appreciable changes made. The lobby of the Fairmont Hotel in San Francisco is largely the way Mrs. Draper envisioned it over forty-five years ago, with Victorian tufting and fringe, Italian rococo mirrors, and a carpet patterned with scrolls that might have appealed to Belle Watling.

Dorothy Draper sold her business in 1960. She died nine years later, at the age of eighty. She had been on the covers of *Time* and *Life* magazines; Edward R. Murrow's cameras had rolled into her apartment at the Carlyle, to which she moved when she left the Hampshire House. Her name was a household word and, since fame was what she wanted above all else, her success was pretty great. A commanding figure, Dorothy Draper dominated her era. If her career had begun in our own times, I can't imagine what she would have done. Perhaps she would have been a television anchorperson, setting everyone straight. I'm sure she wouldn't have been content to be merely one out of the thousands of decorators and designers working today. She needed space and a very big spotlight and she was lucky to have been a star for a long, long time.

William Pahlmann

I F ONE WERE TO COME UP WITH JUST THE right phrase to describe the late Bill Pahlmann, it would probably be "the best-known decorator of his time." He became a household word, as well as an enormous influence on the design world, both commercial and private. He was also the first man to do so—not that one wishes to sound sexist. Before Pahlmann, there had been some very famous ladies in the decorating business who dominated nearly every aspect of the field, most notably the publicity that surrounded it. As we know, publicity has always been a critical element of the decorating world. No one on earth was more adept at keeping herself in the public eye than Elsie de Wolfe. After her, there was Syrie Maugham, who was also brilliant in her ability to occupy center stage. Then, in a far more organized way in a different world (the world of hotels and restaurants),

A snakeskin Victrola with canework panels does sort of catch your eye, but there is a lot more of the fifties evident in this view of William Pahlmann's living room. The color scheme is typical.

137

there came Dorothy Draper, one of whose best clients was Ben Sonnenberg, the Wilbur Wright of publicity. With his help and her formidable drive, Mrs. Draper made herself and her business known to people all across the United States, continuing the tradition of domination by strong women in the decorating field. But sooner or later a Siegfried figure was bound to arrive upon the scene. His name was William Pahlmann. Thirty-five years ago, anyone in America remotely interested in decorating would have known immediately who he was.

The story of his early life reads like a version of the screenplay for *State Fair*. He was born in a little town in Illinois in 1900. When he was six years old, his father died, and three years later his mother packed up her four children (William was the youngest) and moved to San Antonio, Texas, where she ran a boardinghouse. While he was still very young, Pahlmann's talent for drawing was apparent, and his design instincts made enough of an impression for the Prospect Hill Baptist Church to entrust him with the arranging of flowers for special occasions. The jobs he held after high school ranged from working in a shipyard and for a tobacco company to being an automobile dealer. In 1923 he became a traveling salesman for a sewer pipe company. With lots of free time in hotels on the road, he subscribed to a mail-order course in interior design which resulted in his decision to become an interior decorator. Four years later he had saved enough money to go to New York, where he enrolled in the Parsons School of Design, further supporting himself by working in the casts of two Broadway musicals, *Good News* (1927) and *Follow Thru* (1929). His part-time Broadway career was possible because Bill Pahlmann was tall and very good-looking, qualities that made him better fitted to Broadway shows than to selling sewer pipe. His real path, however, and he already knew it, lay in the field of interior decorating.

The Parsons School has played an enormous role in the history of decorating in the United States. Many of the best decorators have been trained there, and its program of study in Paris was a seminal experience for a large number of the students who were lucky enough to take part in it. In 1930, Pahlmann hung up his part-time dancing shoes and went to Paris for a year. When he returned, he opened his own interior decorating business. For a few years business was slow but in 1933 the first Mrs. William Paley (now Mrs. Dorothy Hirshon), a woman of great style whose love of decoration and design was as strong as her husband's, hired Pahlmann, whom she had met and found charming, to do the scaled, working drawings of a mirrored bed she had in mind. The bed still exists and is in Mrs. Hirshon's house on Long Island, a fact that attests to the client's enduring satisfaction with the man who did the drawings. The word that Mrs. Paley spread about Bill Pahlmann's skill gave a significant boost to his career, and he never forgot it.

Even more important than working for Mrs. Paley was the work he did for the department store, B. Altman & Co., an affiliation that also began in 1933 and that helped to prepare him for the job that became the primary vehicle for his great fame: his position from 1936 to 1942 as head of the decorating and antiques department of Lord & Taylor. There he set out on a phase of his career that reached thousands of people through the immensely popular model rooms that he created for the store. Attendance was huge, and so was the publicity. From then on, the development of Pahlmann's style was followed closely by newspapers and magazines all over the country.

This famous style, which became the epitome of fifties design, embodied the anticlassicism and freedom from the past that characterized the modern movements of the early part of the twentieth century. Its chief focus was on the mixture of unexpected visual elements, creating an effect that editors and writers invariably described as "dramatic," "spectacular," and "daring." Accompanying these eclectic (another word that was constantly applied to Pahlmann's style) assemblages were color schemes of an equally daring and surprising nature: red, orange, sky blue, and lime green, or dark brown, olive green, pale blue, and terracotta. He loved surprises and what Robert Hughes calls the "shock of the new." The Lord & Taylor rooms also had a somewhat surreal quality that calls to mind the crazy abandon of Schiaparelli's clothes and even the decoration done for her by Jean-Michel Frank and Christian Bérard. One wonders what Pahlmann saw during his year in Paris. It is certain that Paris in the 1930s was more exciting to him than the historical aspect of its past, yet he did have a favorite house in France, Malmaison, and his description of Napoleon as a rough diamond from Corsica who loved "deep, forest greens," "powerful, strange red-oranges," and "sharp, exciting green-blues" (all colors that Pahlmann adored) shows a sympathy for the Napoleonic which is nevertheless a bit difficult to understand.

To promote his preference for unusual juxtapositions, he added to the elements of his model rooms the theme of travel. Peruvian, Spanish, Portuguese, and Italian buying trips provided him not only with furniture and accessories but also with found

objects that were turned into something else—wrought-iron gates used as headboards or an enormous brass brazier displayed as a piece of sculpture. Like the movies of the thirties, these rooms must have had a particular appeal for the public, trapped by the Depression and unable to travel.

When the war came, Pahlmann served in the Air Force. He was discharged in 1946 with the rank of lieutenant colonel. I once met a woman in St. Louis who had known him during his Air Force days and who remembered him as a handsome, movie-star-like figure who was loved by all his new friends. When he returned to New York enhanced by the additional glamour of his Air Force years, he opened his own design firm. By all accounts it did extraordinarily well from the very beginning. His style was completely developed. Its various and, at first glance, rather unpredictable qualities suited it ideally to the postwar and post-Depression iconoclastic world that embraced it more enthusiastically than ever.

The Pahlmann look represented everything that was new. Upholstery shapes were streamlined and lowered. Materials being developed for the booming building industry, active after many quiet years, became staples in the Pahlmann design vocabulary. Vinyl floors, wall coverings and fabrics never seen before, Scandinavian furniture, and every conceivable reinterpretation of traditional design appeared bravely juxtaposed in rooms that were notable not only for their colorful boldness but also for their informality. As one would expect, there was a great emphasis on radios, record players, and soon, of course, television sets. If anyone ever made it look backward and dull to restate the old-fashioned principles of decoration, it was Pahlmann, with his doctrine of modernizing everything in a room. He was perhaps the quintessential deconstructionist decorator.

First of all, he was completely comfortable with the postwar architecture that most of us now find repellent. His greatest years of fame and success were when the huge yellow brick Manhattan apartment houses were being built, with their low-ceilinged interior spaces, usually lacking any architectural details. These were the buildings that bore the stamp of William Pahlmann. He decorated many of their lobbies and apartments. When he worked in older buildings, he often covered up the details of the past with paintwork and built-ins that left an impression of newness. A typical example of this approach was the apartment he decorated for Margaret Cousins of Doubleday, who had been the famous editor of *Good Housekeeping*. The walls, ceilings, and most moldings were painted a neutral shade of deep cream, a practice he recommended. Then, floating in front of the walls, with their supporting members hidden from view, he installed partitions covered in sleek wood veneer. Shelving units were installed in a similar way, their invisible supports continuing the feeling of floating elements. The shelves, however, were finished not in veneer but in tortoiseshell lacquer, which was repeated in the frame of the sofa, a piece that was half Danish Modern and half studio couch, to dredge up a couple of terms from the period. Next to the tortoiseshell bookcases was a wall panel painted robin's egg blue on which were hung a wide variety of small pictures, two of which (a pair of nineteenth-century portraits) had hung years before in Pahlmann's own living room. The floors were stained almost ebony color, a shade that contrasted boldly with a large ivory and brown Moroccan rug woven

In this brownstone parlor, Pahlmann's eclectic approach is clearly stated. The various elements are not only different, they are also very bold.

in a traditional diamond pattern. There were French and Spanish tables, some rustic, some not. A pair of Louis XV fauteuils, squarely lined up the way he always placed pairs of chairs, were covered in malachite-green damask. Coral and blue-green in varying shades covered the rest of the furniture and the pillows. Oriental and European objects were combined in a way new in the forties and fifties. Rather than evoking the China trade collections of the eighteenth and nineteenth centuries, a tradition so familiar to our eyes, Pahlmann's assemblages and the bold way he arranged them broke from the past, creating instead an impression of surprise and contemporary freedom from stuffy dogma. One gathers that he didn't want to deal with old-guard grandeur in any way. While George Stacey, Eleanor Brown, and Ruby Ross Wood (with her assistant Billy Baldwin) were busy with their killer-chic clients up and down the eastern seaboard, Bill Pahlmann was expanding his company to handle not only the dozens of moderately sized apartments he decorated in Manhattan but also the commissions for houses he executed all over the country, especially in Texas. On top of all this was his burgeoning business in commercial design, which encompassed clubs, offices, and hotels in addition to product designs for various manufacturers. He wrote a syndicated newspaper column called "A Matter of Taste." His restaurant designs were famous, especially the Forum of the Twelve Caesars. He was even a consultant for the Four Seasons in New York. My first memory of a Pahlmann job is the lobby of a hotel in Indianapolis he redecorated in the fifties, in which he combined exaggeratedly elongated sofas, modern boxy versions of tufted Chesterfield models, covered in grey velvet with Louis XVI open-arm chairs finished in silver leaf and upholstered in metallic grey leather. The outside backs of the chairs were covered, alternatingly, in royal blue, emerald green, and crimson raw silk, while the pillows on the sofas were made of the same three colors. In front of each sofa stood a row of small cocktail tables, like those in front of banquettes in an Islamic palace. This sort of table enjoyed a brief vogue owing to Pahlmann's influence. The walls of the lobby, by far the chicest in Indianapolis, were painted anthracite grey with white moldings.

This vivid style was just as apparent in his residential work as it was in his commercial designs. Like Dorothy Draper, his predecessor in the realm of offices, hotels, and restaurants (but not private work, which she chose largely to ignore), Pahlmann saturated his rooms with a sense of uninhibited newness. There were no regional references. His rooms, whether in Texas or Florida or Manhattan, had a similar informality and an almost exotic feeling of world travel and shopping sprees in distant bazaars, which of course is exactly what he did. The customer, he once said, is *not* always right. On the contrary, he's usually wrong. But as long as Pahlmann could keep children and cats (two phobias) at bay, he could guarantee an atmosphere of lively, unconventional modernity where dinner jackets and finger bowls were less common than television and cashmere cardigans. And because he was handsome and charming and part of the nation-wide publicity machine that reported on the nationally known figures in the decorating world, his stamp was sought after by the widest possible range of editors, clients, and manufacturers from one coast to another.

When he retired to Mexico in his mid-seventies, the trends in decorating were changing radically. There was high tech at one end of the scale and the romantic revival of old-fashioned country-house luxury, the style of Sister Parish, at the other. Moving rapidly into view was the even more opulent kind of decoration practiced by Denning & Fourcade, Renzo Mongiardino, and Geoffrey Bennison. But Pahlmann had occupied the position of most famous decorator for a long time and, while on that pinnacle, he made more Americans aware of the decorating and design business than had ever been so before. In many ways, he re-revolutionized the business that Elsie de Wolfe had started a generation before, and turned it into a recognized industry that would never again be dominated by the elegant ladies who had ruled the world of interior decorating for so long.

John Fowler

A T A TIME WHEN BOOKS ABOUT DECORATION appear at the rate of about one a week, no firm is mentioned as often as Colefax & Fowler, the London establishment that began in the thirties when John Fowler joined forces with Sibyl Colefax to create what became the most significant decorating concern in England in this century. Lady Colefax was one of two remarkable partners who sometimes overshadowed John Fowler, at least in the minds of the socially preoccupied public who form the sieve through which most decorating talk passes. The other is Nancy Lancaster, the unsurpassed doyenne of decorating style in England (one might say in America as well, since she was born here and has had an incalculable influence on her Amerian friends and followers). But more of these two formidable women later.

John Fowler was born in 1906. His father deserted his family

The Bruces' entrance hall at Winfield House in London, with a carefully orchestrated view through to the family dining room, epitomized the color philosophy of John Fowler. The portrait of Thomas Jefferson is by William Beechey, after Sully.

when Fowler was little, leaving a wife and two sons to get along on their own. Mrs. Fowler was sympathetic toward her younger son's artistic talents and interests. When he had to leave his school, just before his seventeenth birthday, Fowler worked, unhappily, first for a printer, then for an estate agent in London. After these gloomy jobs, he spent a year working on a cousin's farm in Kent, an experience that confirmed his love of the country and of working in the soil. Chester Jones, in his book on Colefax & Fowler, credits this year on the farm for many of the simple, old-fashioned influences that were to shape the taste of John Fowler, whose love of "humble elegance" continued to prevail in his work even at its grandest.

His next two jobs, probably the result of his mother's help, were momentous in their effect on his career. First, he worked for Thornton Smith, a London decorator, for whom he did decorative painting. Here he learned to restore old Chinese wallpaper as well as to paint new versions, a skill that would have a lasting effect on his renowned ability to deal with paint in a way that enabled him to achieve effects of age on surfaces of all sorts. After Smith, Fowler went to work for Margaret Kunzer, an antiques dealer and decorator whose most imporant client was the home furnishings store, Peter Jones. When Miss Kunzer was asked by people at Peter Jones to set up a painting studio for the store in 1931, it was the twenty-five-year-old John Fowler who headed it up. His experience in painting furniture and objects expanded and increased during the next three years, and by the time he was twenty-eight he decided to leave Peter Jones and open his own studio with his faithful assistants. That was in 1934, and from then until the time he went into business with Sibyl Colefax, four years later, his career expanded from that of a painter of furniture and wallpaper to that of an interior decorator with a fresh and original point of view and a partner who was part of a world, although not unknown to John Fowler, where he was not yet the figure of significance he would soon become.

Sibyl Colefax, a generation older than Fowler, had entered the decorating field in 1933 only as a result of having to make money in the midst of the Depression. Hers was not a career resulting from a lifetime of study and practice. One gathers that she was never a close companion to John Fowler, her sense of social superiority no doubt governed her behavior. Before becoming a decorator, she had been known as one of the most ambitious hostesses in all of London, entertaining constantly at Argyll House, her beautiful brick house in the King's Road which is still the loveliest Georgian landmark in the neighborhood. And just a few doors away lived her friend and rival, Syrie Maugham.

It is important to consider these two women and their taste in relationship to the completely different philosophy of John Fowler. Mrs. Maugham, twenty-seven years older than Fowler, was known for her contemporary way of dealing with decoration. Grand architecture played almost no role in her work. She stripped things down, removing moldings from rooms and finishes from furniture. Her love of pale rooms is well known. They were, in addition to their paleness, urbane and showy. The romantic life of the English cottage did not enter into her work. Lady Colefax, who possessed fine taste, was nevertheless equally uninspired by the sweetness of country life, going in for a more sedate kind of decorating, limited, in Chester Jones's words, to "arranging furniture, designing curtains, lampshades and supplying Wilton wall-to-wall carpeting." But John Fowler's qualifications were different and so was his personal taste. He was an artist. His eye, trained by years of painting, was alert to color in a way that was, looking back over the history of his career, superior to anyone else's. In the Richard Fisher biography of Mrs. Maugham, John Fowler is said to have considered Syrie's color palette a limited one, consisting of navy and white for masculine rooms, blue or pink and white for feminine rooms, and green and white for living rooms. But, to Fowler, color was an unlimited territory, a vast area throughout which he was comfortable. Equally vast was the range of furniture styles that captured his fancy. Although his early preoccupation was with Regency furniture (an unusual taste at the time), his passion for painted country pieces, as well as for French chairs and English chairs in the French taste, was continuous throughout his career. The appearance of dark brown wood in his rooms was always limited, but he never eliminated it altogether. And the extensive span of the Gothic Revival style provided him with an inexhaustible supply of accents that always appeared in a lighthearted way, never in the lugubrious mood of a Victorian clergyman. Whether in the spirit of the mid-eighteenth-century Strawberry Hill or the nineteenth-century Regency Brighton Pavilion, said to have been a revelation to Fowler, the Gothic pieces he used were almost always painted and whimsical. If I had to name one distinction that John Fowler's work possessed, regardless of its degree of richness, since he could be very simple and also very grand, I would say that it was its lightness, both in tone and in weight. Without this quality, he could not have attained the level of gracefulness that invariably kept his rooms from being too rich. Nor were they ever vulgar, a quality he obviously couldn't

John Fowler's tiny country entrance hall was decorated with a French carpet and console table, a gothic chair, and a fancy George III curtain pelmet. Lots of planters and a muted color scheme created a calm effect that his rooms usually possessed.

stand. It is hard to define vulgarity nowadays, when it has been absorbed into practically every phase of modern life, but sixty years ago the old-fashioned distinctions were quite clear, and John Fowler revered those English domestic traditions which reached from the distant past to the present day. His creations were always informed by his love of the past, although he was never shackled by history. He was inspired by it, not enslaved. One of his passions was for "undisturbed houses." They provided him with an ideal. From that point, he could make enormous leaps into the present without allowing the viewer to know where history left off and his work began.

In his personal taste, Fowler was completely suited to the job of decorating English houses of practically any century because he loved all kinds of furniture, even though his preferences were for the years from William Kent and the 1730s through the Regency period. Admittedly, he felt free to lighten anything and everything with his skillful paintbrush. His earliest rooms in the King's Road contained painted chairs, tables, and planters (always a huge range of planters) from many different periods; there was even a Swedish console table in one of the early photographs of his showroom, the sort of table that we think of as being a recent discovery of the contemporary antiques dealer.

Because early English houses invariably had furniture and decoration from the eighteenth century added to their rooms, and later houses contained eighteenth-century pieces brought along from previous places (at least one can indulge in this fiction, if it *is* one), John Fowler was able to edit out what he didn't like in favor of what he *did* without leaving the impression of an old room spoiled by modern insensitivity. He was fantastically sensitive, and he was a romantic. Yet he was not afflicted with that love of twee things that often (indeed usually) goes with a romantic, cottagey taste.

In a more sweeping way, one could say that John Fowler possessed the same qualities of taste that also propelled Elsie de Wolfe out of the Victorian era. He was also struggling against the added new demon of polite, boring taste awash in celadon green and dull, patternless carpets and materials. What existed in the way of color in traditional decorating when he began his career was a range from very dark to a somewhat blah, albeit lighter, approach. This was the climate that inspired Syrie Maugham as well. She, however, began in a radical way and calmed down over the years. John Fowler became more radical and exciting as he grew older. He was inspired to move assuredly along this path by Nancy Lancaster. Mrs. Lancaster entered his life about 1946 (she was Mrs. Ronald Tree at the time), when her husband persuaded her to buy the business of Colefax & Fowler from Lady Colefax. John Fowler, astoundingly, never actually owned any of the business that bore his name.

Much has been written about Nancy Lancaster and John Fowler and how their relationship worked, how they shopped at a time when incredible bargains existed, how the prettiest things went to Mrs. Tree's (later Mrs. Lancaster's) houses, and how they quarreled. During the years immediately after the Second World War, very little money was made; some years, there was a deficit. But together they made gigantic waves in the world of interior decorating.

At the time they became partners, Mrs. Tree was soon to leave the fabled house, Ditchley, where she and her husband had made the eighteenth-century rooms of James Gibbs into unforgettable examples of comfort and beauty. I say the house was unforgettable because so many brilliant people who stayed there never forgot it. Without ever actually being an interior decorator, i.e., going through the day-to-day drudgery of doing other people's houses, Nancy Lancaster has always been a unique catalyst in the world of houses and decorators. Her mother was one of the five Langhorne sisters from Virginia whose charm and style made them famous. One of Mrs. Lancaster's first cous-

The drawing room at Daylesford when the Rothermeres lived there was a textbook of Fowlerisms. The splendid curtains were particularly characteristic of his full-blown style.

ins recently said to me that, whatever the Langhorne charm was, Nancy was loaded with it. I saw her at Stratford Hall in Virginia, a house she adores, discussing fine points of painting with some of the other trustees of the place. The topic being discussed was difficult to resolve. An "expert" was sure he had the only answer. It didn't sound beautiful to Mrs. Lancaster. The hilarious way she debunked the whole controversy was delightful. Everyone (the expert was absent) clearly loved Mrs. Lancaster, her wit, her style, and her idea. These qualities had trailed along after her from one beautiful house to the next and from one decorator after another—e.g., Mrs. Bethall and Stéphane Boudin. Now, as the owner of a decorating firm headed by a man nine years her junior and soon to be the undisputed prince of English decorators (in the Duchess of Devonshire's words), Nancy Lancaster set out with John Fowler to revolutionize English and American decorating, whether they knew it or not.

Leaving Ditchley meant that Mrs. Lancaster needed a new house, and in a few years she found one, Haseley Court. One of her old friends who saw it with her when it was waist-high with overgrown grass remembers her astounding vision of what it would be like when it was completed. By all accounts, it was, following the glories of Ditchley, another high-water mark in comfort and beauty in English country-house decoration. Both Chester Jones in his history of Colefax & Fowler and John Cornforth in his extensive writing on the subject of Mrs. Lancaster and Mr. Fowler have described how the two of them combined an existing collection of furniture and paintings with truckloads of new acquisitions to make Haseley into a romantically colorful and moody house. Never dark and fusty, but also never hard and new-looking, the rooms in Mrs. Lancaster's new house were distinguished by the complex ingredients that made the mature work of John Fowler refreshingly beautiful. The house itself is complex, comprising a Gothic wing, an early eighteenth-century core, and a later Georgian stone facade that presents a deceptively severe face to the world. The architectural backgrounds were enhanced by skillful paintwork, sometimes bold, sometimes subtle. Furniture and paintings were combined with an original, delightful disregard for convention, yet in a way that seemed thoroughly believable given the traditions of English decorating with its history of collecting and accretion. And then there were the elaborately refined details of execution, the trimmings and finishing touches on the curtains, the furniture, and the beds. Whether he was looking at the eighteenth-century clothing at the Victoria and Albert Museum or studying the drawings of Daniel Marot (1660–1752), the widely influential French-born architect-decorator who worked for William of Orange both in Holland and in England, John Fowler continually absorbed information that would inspire his designs. Although he was never interested in recreating an atmosphere of despotic richness, he still favored a detailed kind of execution that involved an almost reckless disregard for the amount of time (and money) required to do all the pinking, ruching, and sewing. He said that he liked things that looked simple but cost a mint. Though by "simple," one mustn't think of minimalism, the Fowler lightness prevented even his richest concoctions from looking overbearing. The most famous room at Haseley (and many of its rooms were learned by heart by those who loved decorating) was the Gothic bedroom in the earliest part of the house decorated for Nancy Lancaster's aunt, Lady Astor. Mrs. Lancaster and John Fowler removed most of the stuffy later Gothic excrescences and transformed the room into an essay on trompe l'oeil, fairy-tale comfort and delicious, frothy color. The contents of this ravishing peachy terra-cotta and off-white room were inconceivably varied. Painted leather chinoiserie screens, a Regency settee, a very ornate *lit à la polonaise,* four wonderful, big Gothic armchairs (which now stand in the Washington drawing room of Mrs. David Bruce, covered in the same material from their Haseley days), two Victorian gilt bronze chandeliers, a couple of French chairs, a huge Bessarabian carpet, odd tables and torchères with rococo and Regency carvings, and a black and gold painted desk. Lastly, carved stag's-head trophies with real antlers hung over console tables on either side of the chimney, a reminder perhaps of the antlers at Ditchley that dated from the time of James I. The exquisite trompe l'oeil, consisting of panels, moldings, and faux plaster relief painted in John Fowler's pretty whites and several shades of the peachy-melon family, was painted by Fowler himself and a new member of his staff, Mr. George Oakes, a man who has had a profound role in the development of the Colefax & Fowler style over the past thirty-five years. It seems to me that the far-ranging skill with which the Colefax firm tackled the recoloring of carpets, chintzes, and wallpapers, not to mention their extensive and elaborate paintwork on jobs of every variety, was greatly supported by John Fowler's and George Oakes's ability to paint. Their authority over the broad topic of paint was in every way exceptional. James Smart, a London painter whose first sophisticated training was under Stéphane Boudin, says that, even taking into account Boudin's genius for color, John Fowler was still the supreme master where painting was concerned. His views on the arrangement of furniture were distinctive and a little unpredictable as well, and in this realm Nancy Lancaster also excelled, an ability that only made the rooms they did together more exciting.

Their next great triumph together after Haseley was the suite of rooms upstairs at the Colefax & Fowler offices in Brook Street that they turned into a flat for Mrs. Lancaster. The centerpiece of this apartment was the great yellow drawing room, which had been designed by Sir Jeffry Wyatville, the architect of Windsor Castle as we know it, in 1821 for his own use. Everything about the room was dramatic, yet there was no trace of flashy decoration; wild, yes, but not flashy. When I saw it in the mid-sixties, it was impossible to say how old the decoration was, but from every point of view it was both beautiful and exciting. Tall and long (16′ × 40′ × 20′ tall), with a shallow barrel-vaulted ceiling, it had walls painted a vivid yellow and then varnished to a high gloss, the varnish adding to the glow of the yellow. The three windows were curtained in yellow silk taffeta, the two end ones draped and trimmed with cords and tassels elaborately swagged, the center one headed with heavy fringe, and all three sets of curtains hanging from gilded poles. At Haseley, the three drawing-room windows were curtained with a contrasting design in the center, an idea that always fascinated Albert Hadley, with his love of ingenious and unexpected design details. Three huge Venetian glass chandeliers hung from the ceiling, the center one differing from the two at the ends. Eventually, the big Elizabethan portraits of the Fitton sisters from Haseley (which now hang in the New York drawing room of Oscar and Annette de la Renta) flanked the fireplace, with later portraits in William Kent frames opposite them. There were six bookcases, four tall and two low. Most of the books were bound in shades of red. Over the tall bookcases hung four Venetian mirrors from the Gothic bedroom at Haseley. In the recessed bay of the center window stood a boulle *bureau Mazarin*, in front of which were a pair of white and gold Regency chairs. Elsewhere in the room were large overstuffed chairs, two Louis XVI bergères, a pair of Georgian open-arm chairs, four Regency chairs with gilded lions' heads at the arms, a tiny Victorian chair, and one from the Régence period at the Louis XVI desk behind

Nancy Lancaster's gothic bathroom at Haseley was a witty profusion of Victorian motifs. Under anyone else's guidance, it would have been a confusion of bits and pieces.

the sofa. A pair of small banquettes flanked the center window. Pictures stood on easels. The upholstery materials were in the reds and off-whites taken from the Bessarabian carpet as well as the Old Rose chintz, which was John Fowler's favorite. In most large Colefax & Fowler rooms there is a skirted table, sometimes more than one. In this yellow masterpiece (for it surely was one), the cloth-covered round table was placed between the overstuffed chairs. Its heavy red wool fringe related to the touches of brilliant red throughout the room. To be able to live in this glorious room and to feel at ease at the same time required a personality with all the dashing qualities of Mrs. Lancaster. It is easy to imagine the influence all this had on her New York friend, Sister Parish.

For himself, John Fowler, with his love of music, gardening, and delicious food, created an equally personal background, one which also reflected his many-faceted decorating philosophy. The house where he created this enchantment was built in the mid-eighteenth century as a folly to be seen in the distance. It is primarily a Gothic Revival facade of red brick, behind which the cottage, with its tiny rooms, was reworked by Fowler to provide the necessary spaces for his country life of, alternatively, solitude and weekend entertaining. Curtains with Gothic pelmets, mirroring the shape of the windows themselves, the Mauny wallpapers he loved, an unpredictable mixture of French and English furniture, and everywhere the formal still lifes he arranged using disarmingly informal elements. Outside, the garden he planned and planted illustrates his love of French formality but, as with everything at the Hunting Lodge, as it is called, the diminutive scale serves to eliminate any trace of yawning pomposity. Facing each other on an axis at a right angle to the main sweep of the design are two little pavilions, inside one of which is still a painted wall I was told was a dry run for the Gothic bedroom at Haseley. On a warm, peachy terra-cotta background he painted, in grisaille, branches of oak resembling the plant forms from a Chinese wallpaper. For all the spontaneity of John Fowler's handiwork, he was never one for dense clutter. Major juxtapositions were the most important elements, and of course a wealth of little details. But little *things* did not fill the surfaces. Backing everything up was a terrific symmetry.

His work could, without question, be grand. Cornbury Park in Oxfordshire, on which he worked with Philip Jebb, one of his favorite architects, is everything that a big country house should be, yet with all its large-scale, luxurious rooms, nothing seems dark or crowded or ponderous. It is flooded with a quality of light and lightness, with scintillating drama at the windows with their typically Fowleresque curtains dripping with ruffles, rosettes, bows, edgings, and trims of all sorts. Curtains like these were always a tour de force in Fowler rooms. They staggered all who saw them, and they sent every New York decorator who worked in a traditional idiom rushing to the curtainmaker in hopes of reproducing something close to the John Fowler look. Let me tell you, those hopes were usually not fulfilled. But just think of the role models: in two Albany apartments (to name one London building), Mr. Fowler succeeded in achieving levels of curtain mania that have become classics. One is the apartment of Baron and Baroness Philippe de Rothschild with its drawing-room curtains of ivory silk hanging in deep points, tied back with bows and lying in piles on the floor. These curtains were made three times before the desired effect was achieved, according to Chester Jones. "I want to feel as though I were in Leningrad," said Pauline de Rothschild to John Fowler. Together they turned a small, fairly nondescript flat into one of those expressions of individuality and chic that occur now and then and influence decoration for years to follow. Similarly, and in the same building off Piccadilly, Fowler decorated the rooms belonging to Mrs. David Bruce and, like the projects they had worked on together before, the results were classic Fowler designs long remembered (and imitated) by all who saw them. Because Mrs. Lancaster was also a great friend of the Bruces, the interplay between them was terrific. I remember seeing the United States ambassador's residence in Regent's Park in the late sixties during the Bruces' time there. The large, rather ungainly house, built by Barbara Hutton in the thirties, was transformed by Fowler and the Bruces from its clumsy self into a vivid interpretation of a country house where plants, flowers, and strong colors were arranged in enchanting juxtapositions. In the hall, apricot-colored walls with yellow curtains edged in red fringe framed the view into the yellow family dining room on one side and the vast drawing room filled with reds, browns, and acid greens on the other. The dark brown oak paneling in the Ritz Hotel-style Louis XV library was daringly painted and picked out in numerous shades of the putty-colored off-whites so closely associated with Fowler. This, along with his love of French details, the tapestry-covered gilt chairs, and Aubusson carpet, gave the harmony of a Boucher to the formerly dreary room.

This was the late part of his career. His activity with Colefax & Fowler was diminishing for two reasons: his health was declining and he was increasingly involved in the expanding project that occupied his last years: advising the National Trust on the restoration of various houses. There have been various criticisms of this phase of John Fowler's career. The decision to hire the most fashionable decorator in the land was in some quarters controversial. Then there was the current view of historical preservation which seeks to justify every decision with the unassailable conviction that it would originally have been done *only* one way. John Fowler's decision to paint the dark brown wood-grained staircase at Sudbury white stirred up just the sort of controversy that plagues many restorations. It is said that there was evidence that it had *been* white. Now no one knows. As with the Schleswig-Holstein debate, those who knew were either dead, insane, or had forgotten. In any case, Sudbury, a house originally begun in 1665 and completed thirty years later, is, in the opinion of many, a more beautiful place today because of John Fowler. I remember the great delight caused by the colors as they progressed from room to room—the strong pink of the hall leading to the yellow and white of the stair hall, the whites upstairs highlighting several distinct periods of plasterwork in different areas, and the soft, creamy pinks of the long gallery.

There was always an overall plan, a program, in Fowler's work. Whether in the immensely grand rooms of the Claremont Club or the miniature spaces of the Hunting Lodge, one could sense the work of a master whose vision, broad and informed, bore the confident stamp of conviction. His great taste, his passion, and his numerous skills set him free to work in any number of modes. They also set him apart from all the others.

Stéphane Boudin

MERICAN DECORATING BEGAN TO ABSORB French influences in the late eighteenth century, and if Thomas Jefferson had been the only American to go to Paris and fall in love with the French neoclassical style, it would have been enough. But he was followed by many others and shortly by another President, James Monroe, whose gilt Empire furniture bought for the White House still reminds us of the high esteem felt for French design and craftsmanship, and for the entire range of French fashion and style that Americans have never ceased to admire. To see, still in place in a Natchez, Mississippi, drawing room, the carpets, wallpaper, and suites of furniture purchased in Paris a hundred and forty years ago is to understand the time-honored allure of shopping in France. Visiting the Breakers, the great Vanderbilt mansion in Newport, where the French firm of Allard & Cie executed one of their many American commissions in the late nineteenth century, one realizes how important it was to many people to be able to boast about having decorations from Paris, even if the upstairs of the Breakers was done by an American, Ogden Codman. Codman was, along with his friend Elsie de Wolfe, a slave to the classical standards of French taste and craftsmanship. Yet it was a slavery they found liberating—from the heaviness and oppression of Victorian decoration.

Our attitude toward French decoration has fluctuated over the years. But one man in particular defined a kind of French taste that continues to represent a standard of refinement and finished perfection that is associated with no other country, whether you are dealing with decoration, clothing, or food. His name was Stéphane Boudin and for over forty years he created and supervised the execution of rooms all over the world that were considered the height of taste and grandeur by royalty and the very rich everywhere. Boudin (he was always known just by his last name) was born in 1888, the same year as Frances Elkins and just a year apart from Rose Cumming and Dorothy Draper. His father was a manufacturer of passementerie, and Boudin, in his thirties, met the founder of Jansen, where he went to sell his father's no doubt exquisite trimmings. This small, charming young man impressed Monsieur Jansen with his talent for design, detail, and proportion. So in 1923, at the age of thirty-five, Boudin went to work for the firm of Jansen, where he stayed until his retirement in the 1960s. Ten years after Boudin joined the firm, Chips Channon, the American expatriate and diarist who lived all his adult life in the thick of London society, was referring to him as "the greatest decorator in the world." With

a reputation like that, it is easy to understand why the Channons hired him to work for them. The assignment was to design their dining room at 5 Belgrave Square, a room that was based on another in the little Amalienburg pavilion in Munich, which was designed in the 1730s by François de Cuvilliés, a Frenchman who spent his life working in various parts of Germany. "It will shock and perhaps stagger London and it will cost us over £6000," wrote Chips a month after his first meeting with Boudin in the summer of 1934. Think, if you will, what £6,000 meant in 1934! Indeed, the room must have astonished everyone, with its silver-gilt carvings and palatial atmosphere. Boudin, with his broad interests and extensive knowledge, had a fascination for German interpretations of French decoration. Thirty years later, he would rely on another Munich room—this time in the Residenz—as the inspiration for his redecoration of the Blue Room in the White House.

In the same decade, Boudin worked on two other renowned houses in England: Ditchley, for Mr. and Mrs. Ronald Tree, and Leeds Castle, for Lady Baillie. Chips Channon and the Trees were all born in America; Lady Baillie's mother was an American. Boudin's most famous client of all, the Duchess of Windsor (he called her "my duchess"), was one of the most conspicuous Americans of her time. The message is clear: Boudin was destined to have an enormous American following.

Mrs. Ronald Tree, who went on to become Nancy Lancaster, the partner of John Fowler and a commanding figure in the world of interior decoration in our time, seems with her Virginia upbringing and her anglophile taste in houses to have been an unlikely client of Boudin's. But the house that she and her husband bought was very well suited to the Boudin vision of splendor, which did not, however, preclude comfort. Although Mrs. Lancaster confided to John Cornforth that Boudin did not see the point of William Kent's decoration, he certainly did see the point of the Italianate interiors designed at Ditchley by James Gibbs, an eighteenth-century architect who had studied with Carlo Fontana in Rome and whose sense of the baroque was highly developed. With a plentiful use of red and gold and a splendid mixture of French and English furniture, Boudin helped to create a series of interiors that were for all who saw them, unforgettable. One of the people who saw them and never forgot was Russell Page, at the time a young landscape architect. A few years later he would form a professional relationship with Boudin, and together they worked on houses throughout Europe.

A much longer time was spent by Boudin on the decoration of Lady Baillie's Leeds Castle, where he worked for almost thirty years. There, in a largely medieval setting, he devised schemes of interior decoration that included furniture from France and England, primarily of the eighteenth century, combined with the richly detailed curtains and bed hangings that were a trademark of the Boudin style. Another of his design strengths everywhere apparent in Leeds Castle is his superb way with color and the finishing of paneled walls. The London painter James Smart worked for Boudin at Leeds and, from him and the painters he brought from France, Jim learned techniques of coloring walls that achieve effects not only of great beauty but also of convincing antiquity. One of these remarkable methods of finishing paneling involves applying gesso to the wood and then, when it has dried to a chalky surface, tinting the gesso with powdered pigment. It was Boudin who also drilled into his painters the lesson that a loosely executed imitation of marble was far su-

The New York drawing room of Mr. and Mrs. Winston Guest was somber and serious, emphasizing the importance of the Chinese porcelain.

perior to the nearly perfect but overly finicky techniques often practiced in England. Jim Smart's lovely paintwork in both America and England is a reminder of Boudin's thoroughgoing skill, which could be so demanding that an entire room might be repainted—two or three times—in order to get the color effect he wanted.

In 1938, Elsie Mendl, then in her seventies, hired Boudin to create a pavilion for a circus ball she wanted to give at her house, the Villa Trianon, at Versailles. The "decorator's decorator," one might have called Boudin from then on. Lady Mendl's pavilion was a fantasy of stripes and blackamoors inside and out, with curtains hanging from under a shaped lambrequin, which continued around the top of the walls on all four sides of the room. These lambrequins appear again and again in Boudin's work, always beautifully cut, shaped, and trimmed with passementerie and tassels. There were Wendel lights from the most famous lighting expert of the time, a dance floor on springs, and Constance Spry, the great London florist, flew over for the party to arrange the planeloads of roses that filled the house.

The following year, 1939, Boudin began working for the Duke and Duchess of Windsor in a house on the Boulevard Suchet. Later, in the mill they bought outside of Paris in 1952, with Russell Page working in the garden, he created what the Windsors thought to be country charm. Of that house, Billy Baldwin once said it showed the duchess's "tacky" Southern taste. Billy, no doubt, was grinding an ax; clearly, he was not enamored of his fellow Baltimorean. Other people, however, loved it. I remember the pictures taken in 1954 and I have kept copies of them ever since, as examples of a luxurious and comfortable albeit flamboyant style that, though perhaps overdecorated, was unlike any house I'd ever seen in photographs before. In 1953 the Windsors moved to a large villa in the Bois de Boulogne and there Boudin moved a great deal of the furniture that had been in the Boulevard Suchet house for fourteen years, plus pieces that appear to have come from Syrie Maugham, another decorator who, like Elsie Mendl, had an influence on the duchess. Boudin created with his exquisite details of paint and paneling an atmosphere of grandeur appropriate to the former king and of an elaborateness acceptable to the duchess, whose preoccupation with clothes, decorating, and parties was unceasing. In the hall of the house in the Bois de Boulogne there is a baroque-shaped commode, probably Swedish, which is identical to the one Syrie Maugham had in her drawing room at Chesham Place at the end of her life and no doubt came from her. The walls of this stair hall are marbleized in the subtle, freely painted way that Boudin loved. The drawing room in the Bois de Boulogne house is paneled in pale blue and silver, carved with tassels and ribbons and embellished with odd foliate wall lights. The entire scheme was inspired by a room in the Residenz Palace in Würzburg, another example of Boudin's fascination with German houses. It might also have been his way of striking out in a style not common to the eyes of Parisians. One understands this urge, considering how often the classic designs of French paneling are repeated. John Cornforth has said that this room in the Bois de Boulogne resembled "almost a smart restaurant." The rest of the house was subtler.

Through the duke and duchess, Boudin met many Americans, among them Mr. and Mrs. Winston Guest, who, in the fifties, lived in two marvelous places: one the Carrère & Hastings house called Templeton on Long Island, and the other a vast penthouse built by the Phippses in Sutton Place in New York City. Working with decidedly English architectural backgrounds in both settings, as well as with inherited furniture and decorations of a primarily English nature, Boudin set out to superimpose on all of this Britishness layers of luxury characteristic of his style, giving the rooms a more European feeling instead of the casual looseness we associate with English rooms. In the New York drawing room, huge old sofas were covered in strong, yellow stamped velvet; seventeenth-century Isfahan carpets covered the floor. The Guests' collection of Chinese porcelain was placed on gilt brackets against the George I paneling. Porcelain on brackets occurs frequently in the work of Boudin, notably in the beautiful pale bird's-egg blue dining room at Leeds Castle.

At the same time Boudin was working in New York for Mr. and Mrs. Guest, he set out on a course that was to be even more influential in America—his work for Mr. and Mrs. Charles Wrightsman. Less well known than the Windsors, the Wrightsmans possessed surer gifts in the realm of artistic taste. Charles Wrightsman was, in John Pope-Hennessy's words, a perfectionist who distinguished between the very good and the superlative. He only bought the superlative. With seemingly unlimited money, they began to decorate a house in Palm Beach, Florida, that had been designed by Maurice Fatio. It was a rambling villa that had previously belonged to Mr. and Mrs. Harrison Williams and had been decorated in those days by Syrie Maugham. It was completely changed by Boudin from its thirties sleekness and Mrs. Maugham's London overtones to a richly finished version of a French pavilion overlooking the Atlantic Ocean. Eighteenth-century parquet floors and paneled walls painted ravishing colors typical of Boudin provided the backgrounds for the Wrightsmans' brilliant collection of eighteenth-century French decorative arts. During the same era he decorated the Wrightsmans' Fifth Avenue apartment, where even more astonishing furniture, carpets, and porcelains, not to mention pictures, came and went, often headed for a permanent home in the Wrightsman rooms at the Metropolitan Museum, where, at the end of his life, Boudin installed two great Louis XV rooms, one of which Jansen had bought from a palace in Vienna many years before. Some of the furnishings from that palace had been used by Boudin thirty years earlier in the London dining room of the Channons.

ment is another of those legendary New York dwellings whose owners make up a fascinating list for social study. Over the years it has belonged to Mrs. William Burden, Mr. and Mrs. Charles Payson, and now Anne Bass.

At that same period in the sixties, Boudin was decorating a large, rather cumbersome house newly built for Mrs. Robert Young in Palm Beach. Mrs. Young, a sister of Georgia O'Keeffe, was every bit as strong-willed as her more famous sibling. The furniture for the house was upholstered in muslin and sent to Florida for final approval before being returned to New York and having its permanent covers put on—a touch of perfection and extravagance that few decorators would consider possible.

For Mr. and Mrs. H. J. Heinz, Boudin created a two-story-tall, green velvet room on the East River, above the apartment where Greta Garbo lived. The Heinz drawing room was filled with gilt chairs covered in sky-blue velvet. On the walls hung some of their lovely collection of Impressionist paintings. The overdoors of the room recalled the Italianate baroque overdoors at Ditchley. All the woodwork was painted white with moldings picked out in gold. The familiar Boudin lambrequin ran around the top of the room.

For Gianni Agnelli, Boudin decorated the historic and legendary villa in the south of France designed by Ogden Codman for himself and called La Leopolda. A few years later he worked at Villar Perosa on the Agnelli house outside Turin, creating and restoring, with the inspired help of Mrs. Agnelli, interiors evocative of eighteenth-century Piemontese country-house life. The beds, with their elaborate hangings done in what is called "bandera," a form of embroidery typical of the region, are particularly enchanting, surrounded as they are by rococo plasterwork and furniture. In this lovely eighteenth-century house, owned by the Agnellis for five generations, Boudin's range and abilities were given full scope with correspondingly marvelous results.

The meticulous refinement of these houses, filled with collections of tremendous quality and value, was the result of careful planning. There was not, in this kind of programmed decorating, much room for the odd, accidental intrusions that make romantic old houses so unpredictable and therefore disarming. Boudin's great rooms were splendid. In the European tradition, splendor and frumpiness are rarely compatible, except perhaps in English houses, but Boudin never imitated the casual dowdiness we so often see attempted now. Even his advice on flower arranging was strictly related to the color schemes of the rooms, with the placement of the individual arrangements and their selection of color tonality planned according to the view into the *next* room and *its* color scheme.

Finally, of course, the work that Boudin did in the White House during the Kennedy administration is the most significant for us in the United States, far more so than the tremendously ornate decorations he created for the very, very rich. He was chosen for this assignment over native-born decorators because his European background had accustomed him to working on a monumental scale in great houses of heroic proportions. And, as we have seen, he could adapt himself to the style of any country. At the White House, Boudin arranged rooms in a manner that recalls the nineteenth century, displaying to the best possible advantage the collections of American furniture and paintings that were begun in the sixties.

The oval yellow drawing room on the second floor, the most formal of the rooms in the private quarters, he interpreted as an American room with a French past, recalling the fact that both Jefferson and Monroe lived with simple Louis XVI furniture in the White House. He even placed a Fragonard drawing, *The Apotheosis of Benjamin Franklin,* on an easel in this room (it had been given by the Wildensteins). There were, of course, the Bellangé pieces purchased in Paris by Monroe that Boudin arranged in the Blue Room, for which they had been commissioned, decorating the room around the Empire style of the furniture. It was he who engineered the hanging of paintings in double tiers on the very high walls of the White House. His most controversial room was the Blue Room itself, which he decorated in white silk with a continuous blue swagged lambrequin which, in a way that he liked and often employed, became the valances of the curtains as it moved around below the cornice. This room, inspired by a room in the Residenz in Munich of the same early nineteenth-century period, was apparently misunderstood, because, beautiful though it was, it was changed not many years afterward. His hand, however, can still be seen in the organization of the Red and Green Rooms: the first an Empire parlor featuring the American cabinetmakers Charles Honoré Lannuier and Duncan Phyfe, the latter displaying the more delicate Federal style based on English models popular in the late eighteenth and early nineteenth centuries. His confident arrangement of furniture and paintings vividly evokes the past of this often altered house.

Although many of Boudin's restorations at the White House remain, only one of his rooms has been left exactly as it was, and that is the enchanting brilliant blue and white toile dressing room off the Queen's Bedroom. In it, Boudin assembled a collection of charming black and gold painted furniture, which reminds one more of Madeleine Castaing than of Stéphane Boudin, but it is nevertheless furniture that would be equally at home in France or in the United States. It is a prophetic room insofar as it was the precursor of the later nineteenth-century taste that has since become so popular in the United States. Boudin, more than anyone, could handle styles covering a range from Italy, Germany, and Portugal to nineteenth-century America. His work was an illustration of a powerful combination of taste, historical knowledge, and the bold ability to execute his designs in the most dramatic possible way. Yet he shunned all public view of his private life. Though he was beloved by his clients for his sweetness, modesty, and good humor, he never evinced a desire to move in the fashionable world whose settings he created. His joy was in working with his artisans, with putting into manufacture the historical details he came across, then retreating into his very French and simple private life. Whether staying at the Pierre Hotel in New York or at his home in France, few people ever knew anything about his private taste or how he lived. That was how he wanted it and that was the way he kept it.

George Stacey

A SHORT WHILE AGO I WENT TO SEE A HOUSE in East Hampton decorated by George Stacey nearly thirty years ago for Mrs. William Lord, a woman who has been his friend and client for many years and who lives there all year round now. Its rooms still bear the Stacey stamp of boldly stylized chic that, paradoxically, has aged to a mellowness one rarely finds in fashionable statements from the past. One reason we redecorate so often is to erase the trendy flaws that reflect the unconscious mistakes we make trying to be in style. Twenty-five years or so ago, when this lovely East Hampton house was being done up, there were a lot of popular trends now almost impossible to remember, they've been buried so deep. George Stacey, however, never embraced Mylar wallpaper or chrome and plastic tables. He relied on strong color schemes and carefully selected and arranged

George Stacey's country living room in France, with its rustic beams and tile floor, somehow seems perfectly at home with its much grander furniture. The color scheme is pure Stacey.

pieces of furniture, each one beautiful on its own. Because he is a classicist of sorts, as well as the possessor of a fine and highly trained eye, his choices have survived the years, carrying their beauty with them.

Entering this East Hampton house, one meets a vivid dark green and white color scheme in the hall, which is also an enclosed porch. Since it faces south, the space receives brilliant light that is as powerful as the colors of the room itself. The floors are white. The walls are a dark leaf green. The painted trim and *all* the furniture, some of which is wicker, are white. Two or three pillows are chrome yellow, and that's it. Because George Stacey is constitutionally incapable of incoherent clutter and confusion, the arrangement of furniture and objects is balanced and logical. From this room one enters a high-ceilinged living room in which all the Stacey principles of decorating have been put to use, but on a casual level, appropriate to a shingled house in Suffolk County.

The first impression of the room is one of color, not surprising in the work of a decorator with a decided viewpoint on the subject. If George Stacey had gone in for painting altarpieces, the most important figures would no doubt have been dressed in red and green. The large areas would have been neutral tones of smoky taupe or brown. There would have been shimmering elements of yellow and blue here and there, and over the entire surface patches of gold would have added brilliance and richness. Although this beautiful Long Island room is not the result of any formula, it does indeed represent the Stacey color hierarchy, with its taupe walls and curtains and its dark brown carpet against which the more primary colors stand out. Old, flaky red paint covers the frame of a tall French cabinet from a Louis XV-period

The Stacey free hand is clearly illustrated by this fireplace surround made from an Italian overdoor. Strong colors and rigid symmetry are also typical.

country house. Two chairs at the opposite end of the room are covered in the same red. They flank a French gaming table. The chairs to either side of the red cabinet are covered in a green the color of Fitzhugh Chinese export porcelain. Two beautiful Louis XVI bergères are in old, very cracked brown leather (also very beautiful). Two other Louis XVI chairs are in off-white, between which is a bone-colored sofa. Bright blue glass lamps and yellow pillows contrast sharply against the shadowy background. All around the room, old surfaces—paint, leather, carved wood, brass—counteract the stylish brightness of the color scheme. At one end of the room a pair of tall panels of painted Chinese wallpaper flank a doorway, restating the entire range of colors used in the room. The pictures that share the wall space with the Chinese panels and a beautifully decayed Louis XVI mirror consist of two works by Walt Kuhn and two densely summery landscapes by Sheridan Lord. The balance of old and new elements is strictly even, never tilting either way. The arrangement combines an architectural sense, a sophisticated knowledge of proportion, and the juxtaposition of pieces from different periods and places. Also clearly stated is the concern for conversation and the comfort of those who want to converse. This brings me to a key point in the personality of George Stacey and how it relates to his work.

George Stacey is a man of enormous wit, whose greatest pleasure is to sit and engage in conversation, the kind of chat that usually pokes fun at everything and everybody—except for the serious topics of architecture and decoration, and the stylish people he has worked for all his professional life. His love of amusing and intelligent talk has always guided him in the arrangement of rooms. They have without exception been composed for intelligent habitation. Not for him those glamorous set pieces we know from photographs to be sleek and gorgeous to look at, but murder to sit in. (Does that reflect their creators?) Yet he has always loved glamour, both in people and in decoration.

If you saw George Stacey dressed in his black turtleneck, black coat, and black hat, you might think he was a private detective. And when he reached into his pocket, you would expect him to produce a badge or a revolver, but it would only be for a cigarette, which he would proceed to smoke in a tremendously cool way. His speech, however, is not that of a Dashiell Hammett character, but rather that of a Connecticut Yankee, which is what he is. The only child of two only children, George was born in Stratford, Connecticut, in 1901, where his father owned a lumber mill. All the men in the Stacey family had gone to Yale University. As it happened, neither lumber mills nor Yale appealed to the Staceys' son, who preferred drawing house plans and whose favorite building in town was a Greek Revival ship captain's house with a compass in the newel post. After high school he worked in a Bridgeport decorator's shop and saved his money, a wise practice, because one day an application form arrived from the Parsons School of Design in New York, sent at the request of George's high school English teacher, who had noticed the amount of time he spent drawing houses. Since his father was opposed to design school, George had to go it alone. But after he had been awarded two scholarships, his father was finally won over. One of the scholarships, providing for a semester of study in Paris, came about because the famous Parsons teacher William Odom recognized George's talent and administered a skillful test to determine the quality of the young man's eye. One day, on the pretext of delivering some important school papers, George was summoned to Odom's Fifth Avenue apartment. As he stood looking at its beautiful furniture, George was asked by his teacher what piece he considered best in the room. The precocious student promptly pointed to a commode that must have been the owner's favorite too, because the next words out of Odom's mouth were, "How would you like to spend a semester studying in Paris?" The Stacey answer, undoubtedly laconic, was affirmative. A new epoch in his life was about to begin, an epoch dominated by France and things French. Today, George, who is an incredible ninety years old, is mainly concerned with his upcoming travels to and from France, where he still has a flat in Paris and a house in the country. The preoccupation that began when he took up his studies in Paris nearly sixty-five years ago has continued ever since.

The Parsons School program in Paris was rigorous and thorough; it gave its participants, at least the most intellectually tenacious ones, a deep knowledge of French architecture and decoration. Bicycle trips into the countryside to measure and draw extensive details of châteaux sound more like the activities of John Ruskin and his parents than those of American design students. But that's what Parsons students of two generations ago did, and the effect was lasting. The experience altered George's point of view forever.

Returning to New York, George wanted to work for one person—Rose Cumming, whose personal and professional styles were noteworthy. He got the job but, the way he tells it, it only lasted for one day. He quit after spending eight hours cleaning the cellar. After Rose, he worked briefly for Taylor and

Thirty years ago, George Stacey decorated his château in a style descended from the strict point of view of Ogden Codman. The bookcase on the right is still in his French sitting room.

Lowe, a Madison Avenue decorating firm. The trouble with *that* job was that he was allowed to do nothing but draw. To cheer himself up, he left for France again, where he met Hans Van Nes, with whom he decided to go into the antiques business. The plan was for George to live in Paris, find the furniture, and ship it back to New York. This arrangement worked fine until the Depression, which ended it. But it established the pattern of George's living partly in France and partly in the United States.

It is clear to me, from his own words and from my knowledge of his personality, that George Stacey was not meant to be an employee in someone else's decorating firm. So, with the Great Depression under way and his antiques business finished and not wanting to sweep up for Rose Cumming (or anybody else, for that matter), he set out on his own. Typically, his first client was a chic woman of great attraction, the sort who figures so prominently in the Stacey oeuvre—Mrs. Ward Cheney. She headed a list that would grow to include Mona Williams, all three Cushing sisters, Grace Kelly, and Ava Gardner. Mrs. Cheney was young and stylish and "the funniest woman I ever knew," says the loyal George, still admiring half a century later. Over the years he helped the Cheneys decorate a big new house in Locust Valley, a Manhattan apartment, and a house in Sutton Square. The evolution of his style can be seen in these rooms decorated over a period of twenty years. Although he always loved eighteenth-century French furniture and strong color schemes, the Stacey approach to the mood of a room altered over the years. The Cheneys' early thirties Art Deco house in the country with its beige and silver color schemes had a touch of Hollywood about it. The passage of years saw the increasingly romantic Mr. Stacey place an Edwardian center banquette in the middle of the Cheneys' next drawing room, replacing the semicircular satin sofa and huge, round lacquer coffee table that had been there before. The center banquette (or *borne,* as it is called in France) exemplified George's ability to assimilate Victoriana into his designs. Both Babe Paley and Betsey Whitney tapped this vein for the many rooms he decorated for them during two decades. Some of this tufted luxury evokes Syrie Maugham. I once asked George what he thought of Mrs. Maugham. "I guess I was pretty impressed," was his answer.

Mrs. Cheney's Sutton Square house, with its New York brownstone proportions and its view of the East River, was an expression of the old-fashioned style that has become popular again in the last twenty years. Classic upholstered pieces, scaled down in the manner of William Odom (the Odom chair is named after him), were combined with French and English antiques of various styles. The flowered needlepoint drawing-room carpet was an exception to the long-term Stacey preference for solid-colored carpets. He prefers plain carpet because it does not fight with the lines of the furniture. To him, good furniture takes precedence over everything else. George Stacey never got wrapped up in the architectural renovations that occupy so much of a decorator's time these days. Nor did he pursue the signature look many designers strive to achieve: an instantly recognizable style—the result of constant and highly publicized repetition. The real focus of his style has been good French furniture with bits of English and Italian thrown in. The clients for whom he decorated so many successive houses and apartments were unquestionably grateful to be able to move their precious collections from place to place, watching their value increase all the time.

Before she was married to William Paley and afterward, George did many rooms for Babe Paley, in New York and on Long Island. Because of that work, he decorated a New York

His former New York drawing room had many of the eighteenth- and early-nineteenth-century decorative elements that have filled George Stacey's rooms for over sixty years.

apartment and the famous Stanford White playhouse in Rhinebeck, New York, for Mrs. Paley's sister Minnie and her husband, Vincent Astor, as well as a house or two for Bill Paley's sister and brother-in-law in Philadelphia. He decorated Mr. and Mrs. Averell Harriman's house off Fifth Avenue in addition to parts of the governor's mansion in Albany. Governor Harriman, when George stayed with them in Albany, would introduce him as "Minister of the Interior." Knowing that difficult house very well, I can assure you that its history would have been far happier if George had been placed *permanently* in control.

In 1956, George took a twelve-year lease on the Louis XIII Château de Neuville, located between Versailles and Dreux. There, in rooms of considerable architectural beauty, with stone floors, severe boiseries, and the blunt simplicity of floor plans prior to the nineteenth-century passion for complication, intricacy, and hordes of servants, he put together rooms of "timeless beauty"—a cliché, let me quickly add, that would make him gag. The Victorian quirks he used in apartment decoration were eliminated. His Connecticut Yankee qualities were in control. The admiration he felt for the work of the American expatriate Ogden Codman is apparent. So is his lack of interest in period rooms. Instead, there was the skillful mixture of periods that always exists when collectors of taste combine the things they love regardless of a curatorial concern for dates.

The years he lived in the Château de Neuville were also the years when he worked extensively for Princess Grace and Prince Rainier in Monaco and for Ava Gardner in Madrid. While she was still Grace Kelly, George had decorated her New York apartment across from the Metropolitan Museum. He admired her and he admired her taste, and when in 1956 she married Prince Rainier, George was asked to cheer up the palace, a job that even the difficult Somerset Maugham complimented him on. His work for Ava Gardner covered an even longer period and included two houses and an apartment in Madrid and finally her last apartment in Ennismore Gardens in London. The Madrid drawing-room color scheme was classic Stacey—brown damask sofas, gilt chairs covered in red and in yellow, and walls and curtains in mauvey grey, all of this sitting on top of a white carpet. Her London drawing room had scarlet and forest-green materials used on gilt chairs, white for the sofas and the carpet. Framed panels of scenic antique Chinese wallpaper were worked into the paneling of the room. These were something of an exception. Like highly figured carpets, elaborately patterned wallpaper is, in the opinion of George Stacey, a distraction from the more important issue of good furniture.

He is a decorator whose interests cover an enormous range of styles. A certain kind of taste has always been more important to him than the changing dogma of fashion. His rooms are fashionable because he has a handle on what's chic and because his clients were always so stylish. Mrs. Lord wakes up in East Hampton each morning in an enchanting bedroom redolent of the charm of working for many years with an old friend who is also a great decorator. The room is entirely blue and white. Shaped blue and white trompe l'oeil rococo panels, inspired by a room in Venice, decorate the wall spaces between the four windows and three doors. A white carpet and white shutters at the windows give the room sparkle and work with white-painted bamboo turned tables and étagères filled with shells, and a pair of Victorian dressers, also painted white. There are eighteenth-century French chairs and a poudreuse of the same period, in addition to bamboo Regency chairs, an upholstered chaise longue, and a bed made up in blue and white Porthault linens. Everywhere you look, lamps, objects, and pictures form a coherent collection of beautiful decorative arts. The arrangement is strict and orderly but not spare; the room is too full for that. There is none of that dated quality which spoils so many rooms over time. Bold color schemes (like those of Dorothy Draper) and George Stacey's informed eye for antique furniture and accessories, have enabled him to create rooms where comfort and beauty matter more than any amount of clever monkey business. The kidding around is saved for the conversation, which, after all, is always better in a beautiful room.

Sister Parish

HEN DOROTHY MAY KINNICUTT WAS BORN, the Edwardian period was coming to a close, but it left its mark on Mrs. Parish (as Miss Kinnicutt came to be known). Although she is the most famous American decorator of the present day, the quality that stands out about her more than any other is her old-fashionedness. All of the love of the past that is so in vogue nowadays is simply natural for her. She has been one of the great influences for the last thirty years, and that influence has always led in the direction of the past in general and the Edwardian period in particular. It was a time when late Victorian stuffiness and ugliness were replaced by a new awareness of the eighteenth century, but with a romantic rather than a pedantic view of how things ought to be done. If you think of great Edwardian hostesses as we read about them in Henry James, Edith Wharton,

Mrs. Parish's summer living room in Maine strikes a note of nostalgia that endears her work to people all over America.

or even the reminiscences of Cecil Beaton (and you really would have to refer to *all* of these sources), you can just imagine Mrs. Parish in the setting of luxurious clutter, arranged in a way that shows a delicious combination of great taste and a sort of opulent coziness. Even her presence is Edwardian. While formidably correct and completely fed up with the sloppiness of modern manners, Mrs. Parish can still disarm an entire room with the biting hilarity of one of her stories, always delivered in her sweet, whispering voice, a voice that is almost like a purr. I remember lunching with her and one of her old friends, another creature of great humor and charm, when I had come to New York for the day to buy my wife's engagement ring twenty-seven years ago. "Engagement ring!" they both shrieked in mock astonishment. "What a stupid idea! I sold mine to buy a horse," said Mrs. Parish. "My husband pawned mine to pay a gambling debt," said the friend. There we sat in the Parishes' Seventy-ninth Street dining room with the Italian painted wall panels, the faience vegetables, and the Louis XVI chairs, eating our soufflé and nibbling our salad, talking about engagement rings in terms that would have suited Dorothy Parker. It was pure Sister Parish.

Sadly, one can seldom remember with any accurate detail first meetings. The day I met Albert Hadley and Mrs. Parish, however, is still clear in my memory. I had an appointment to be interviewed by Mr. Hadley, an appointment that had been arranged by the artist Hilary Knight, the creator of the illustrations for *Eloise* and the uncle of a college friend of mine. It was a job interview. Mrs. Henry Parish II (in those days no Inc. or anything after her name) was located in a tiny, immaculate, and completely enchanting suite of offices just off Madison Avenue on East Sixty-ninth Street. The bookkeeping department was hidden away around the corner somewhere. Stepping directly off the street into the hall of Mrs. Parish's office was more like entering a miniature apartment than a place of business. Certainly it was not like an office. On either side of the hall there was a room with windows on the street. The room on the left was Mrs. Parish's; the one on the right, Mr. Hadley's. In the back there was a sample room. A secretary sat in the hall.

My interview with Albert was devoted primarily to looking through my portfolio of drawings and discussing the rooms that had inspired them. Some of the drawings were taken from photographs of real rooms. Albert, whose memory is phenomenal, knew every room that was either depicted or referred to in any way. At the end of our talk he disappeared for a minute. When he came back into the room he asked if I could stay a little longer because Mrs. Parish would like to see me. I said yes, of course, and in I went.

Her office was really a little sitting room. There was no desk in sight. The walls were painted cream color. The upholstered chairs were covered in a Clarence House print (unglazed) with pastel Chinese tree peonies on a taupe-y, no-color ground. The stems and leaves were printed in a watery lettuce green, the color of a Chelsea or Longton Hall leaf plate, the sort of porcelain that exists in all of Mrs. Parish's own rooms. In one of the windows a white porcelain parrot sat on a hoop-shaped perch. A pair of dwarf Louis XVI console tables with matching mirrors (painted white) flanked the door leading out to the hall. They were arranged opposite another mirror that enabled Mrs. Parish to see from her chair who came and went through the front door.

The drawing room of Mrs. Vincent Astor's William Delano house overlooking the Hudson River contains all the references to eighteenth-century France and England that she loves. The sunny, comfortable quality of this huge room dispels any sense of heavy opulence in a way typical of both Mrs. Astor and Mrs. Parish.

It was a blistering June day, and Mrs. Parish had just come down from Maine, which, by the way, is, in her opinion, the single most wonderful place on earth. Her black Humber (a sign of her great anglophilia) was parked outside, and Yummy, the Peke, was drinking from his green glass dish inside the door, waiting to bite the next available ankle or hand. Mrs. Parish was in a severely plain but beautiful navy-blue dress with a high round neck and a short strand of big pearls. They were, I learned later, pop beads, the disconnecting of which she loved to demonstrate. Here is the remarkable part: explaining that she had no time, Mrs. Parish asked whether or not I was free later that day at five o'clock. Free! I was looking for a job and could have met at *any* hour. I said yes. Then, in her soft, high voice, she said to this total stranger just off the street, "I live at 39 East Seventy-ninth Street. If I'm a little late, the key is in the drawer of the hall table." Now, I grew up in a small town where most people were not especially concerned with security, but I was astonished by the plan set out by Mrs. Parish for my arrival later in the day. This was my first hint of how amazing she can be.

At precisely one minute before five, I arrived at 39 East Seventy-ninth Street, went up to the twelfth floor, and, sure enough, had to let myself in. The front door opened into a small, square vestibule that was covered in antique mirror over which natural-colored bamboo fretwork had been painted by Eloi Bordelon (this was before Robert Jackson's arrival in New York the following year). To carry out the Brighton Pavilion mood of this hall, a painted iron lantern in the form of bamboo hung overhead. Off this vestibule, a long, wide hall led past the bedroom to the drawing room at the far end. The walls of this

hallway were covered with panels of old Japanese paper, the background of which was a paper-bag tan color. The design was an all-over jumble of wonderful white flowers and soft green leaves. Mrs. Parish later said that Frank Crowninshield of *Vanity Fair* had called it the "confused style" of Japanese painting, a typical example of the way she has of debunking her things. Once, when asked what she collected, I heard her say, "What do I collect? I collect junk!" Against the Japanese paper stood a set of white painted Louis XVI chairs covered in their original needlework (*not* tapestry) in the same colors as the wallpaper. At the far end, near the arch leading into the drawing room, was a boulle cabinet with the drinks tray on it. This piece still holds the drinks things in her Fifth Avenue apartment; in fact, most of her furniture still exists in one form or another, repainted, regilded, or looking just the same.

Inside the drawing room the floor was shiny and bare, as it always was in the summertime while the Aubusson was out having its annual restoration. All the sofas and chairs were slip-covered in a cotton material printed in a sepia and off-white vermicelli pattern. When I say *all,* I mean a lot of furniture: there were two sofas and a Louis XVI canapé, three large up-holstered chairs, and five or six small ones. Over the Caen stone French mantel hung the glamorous Ned Murray portrait of Mrs. Parish in a gauzy evening dress that still hangs over her drawing-room fireplace. There were huge bowls of carnations in three shades of pink. Battersea candlesticks, English botanical por-celain, and ivory and lacquer objects sat on all the table tops. Late afternoon sunlight streamed through the window, filling the room with bright pools of light and reflecting on the polished floor. When Mrs. Parish and Yummy arrived, we discussed what I would do and when I would begin. I was twenty-three. She has always said she thought I was thirty-five. I must have looked particularly grown up that day, or haggard—I was scared to death.

The following week I reported for work. One of the first things we did, Mrs. Parish and I, was to go around to the various showrooms where I met the people in charge. Mrs. Parish would introduce me as Mr. Hampton in her rather formal way. Looking back, as I often do, I always think of the great good fortune of first encountering the New York decorating world with Mrs. Parish guiding me by the hand.

In the years prior to the sixties, Mrs. Henry Parish II had worked for a lot of people who had no intention of seeing photographs of their houses published in newspapers or magazines. In all the years of my childhood, I remember only three photographs of Mrs. Parish's work. These were of her Sutton Place apartment during the war; a very modernistic, and uncharacteristic, mirrored dining room for Mr. and Mrs. Laurance Rockefeller; and a beach house in Southampton for the daughter of Mrs. Diego Suarez (Mr. Suarez had designed the house). The Southampton house was extremely simple—a real beach house—with wicker chairs and clay pots of geraniums. In the picture of her own apartment, the table in the foreground has on it the melon tureen, the porcelain lettuces, and the leaf plates that have sat on her table for fifty years or more. There is also a terra-cotta nude by Laurence Tompkins, always in view, a blanc de chine lamp, and a copy of the *Harvard Alumni Quarterly*. The "confused" Japanese panels are on the walls. Over the years

This red table and its freight of colorful enamel and porcelain has occupied a spot in Mrs. Parish's drawing rooms for thirty years.

her style has become more embellished, but the sense of permanence, of living with one's things instead of tossing them out every few years, has always prevailed.

Mrs. Parish's work for the Kennedys and the appearance in *House & Garden* of her houses in Maine brought her to the attention of the public in a way that she had never known before. From then on, her fame has only increased. For the last twenty years she has surely been the most famous decorator in America. The reasons are numerous and varied. At the very moment that all the craziness of the sixties—the miniskirt, the geometric Mylar wallpaper, and the Beatles—was bursting on the scene, a completely opposite wave of anglophilia was beginning. Strangely, it was reinforced by the high-fashion presence of Mary Quant, Thea Porter, and David Hicks. The New Wave English and the Old Wave English (Nancy Lancaster, John Fowler, the tailors, bootmakers, and gunsmiths of London, plus all of Bond Street) vied for the attention of fashion-conscious America. Diana Vreeland, the new editor of *Vogue* and an old friend of Mrs. Parish, recorded the whole thing. I believe one can safely say that the Old Wave won out.

Mrs. Parish is very much part of the Old Wave, but her instincts are the sort that place her always firmly in fashion. No sooner did the Op-Pop decorating style get under way than it was completely buried (whether alive or dead, I cannot say) by the chintz and bows of Colefax & Fowler and Mrs. Parish. And the list of clients who hired the firm of Mrs. Henry Parish II, soon to become Parish-Hadley, grew to be more and more fashionable and less and less opposed to seeing their rooms in the pages of *Vogue* and *House & Garden*. In 1963 that list included Mrs. Astor, Mr. and Mrs. Engelhard, and of course the Kennedys.

In a few years it would include the Whitneys, the Paleys, the Reeds, and assorted Rockefellers.

Before Albert Hadley came to work for her in 1962, Mrs. Parish was not known to sweep through a house making architectural changes of any great degree. McMillen, where Albert had worked for five years, was accustomed to altering houses and apartments in order to achieve architectural backgrounds for their proposed decorating schemes. Mrs. Parish, like Billy Baldwin, did not go in for this sort of thing, but with Albert and his bold, architectural approach, everything changed. The new job in the summer of 1963 that most occupied Mrs. Parish and Mr. Hadley was the redecoration of the top floor of the East Sixty-third Street townhouse of Mr. and Mrs. John Hay Whitney, the only significant townhouse to have been built in the years after World War II. The large room on the roof, originally planned as a modern space with lots of glass and beige, had been more or less useless in its severe state and was now being turned into a more traditional, livable sort of place. The first scheme proposed to the Whitneys was one with intricately designed trellis walls, a device well suited to the tiny roof gardens at the top of the house. The trellis idea, however, was rejected; then, in a flash of some kind of brilliance, Mrs. Parish bought an old, flaking pine shutter at an antique shop in Maine and, showing it to the Whitneys, said, "This is what the room should look like." Somehow, they understood. My first assignment was to do a series of drawings showing the room with the window walls covered by floor-to-ceiling flaking shutters. The finished product, which appeared many months later in *Vogue* magazine, showed the deceptively casual mixture of color and furnishings that is so typical of Mrs. Parish's style. In addition to the pine shutters, there were off-white walls, a huge cotton Tibetan rug the color of faded blue jeans, a blurred blue and white print based on a design of crewelwork, rough-textured upholstery materials, and an assortment of Louis XIII, XV, and XVI provincial furniture. The tour de force was the paintings—Rousseau, Utrillo, Braque, and Picasso. The flowers were done in the manner of Dutch seventeenth-century still lifes. An elaborate Italian mantel added to the bold Continental flavor of the decoration, yet the atmosphere was completely American. Even the white paper lampshades, always favored by Billy Baldwin, contributed to the crisp feeling of the present day. Above all, the room achieved the chic, the informality, and the luxurious comfort that its owners wanted.

This informal, luxurious comfort is more evident in the Parishes' Maine houses than anywhere else. These yellow and white houses, one called the Summer house, the other called the Town house (there's no town!) appeared in *House & Garden* in the sixties for the first time. Their overwhelming sense of nostalgia was as enchanting as a Beatrix Potter drawing. Inside, there were green painted floors, organdy tiebacks, and organdy frills tacked to the mantels. Victorian settees and chairs upholstered in chintz mixed with rocking chairs and odd pieces of turn-of-the-century upholstery conveyed the mood of old hand-me-downs that can make us all look with greater love and assurance upon our own things. Twenty-five years ago a lot of owners of new plastic and glass tables must have experienced a pang of longing when they gazed at the pictures of these adorable rooms. Every possible kind of needlework made into pillows,

rugs, chair covers, or doilies testified to Mrs. Parish's deep love of simple handcrafts. There were painted lampshades and doorstops, baskets and Sandwich glass, rag rugs and hooked rugs. And the quilts! I think it's right to give Mrs. Parish a large amount of the credit for the quilt craze that began then. From that time on, an old cottage industry was reborn.

In a very short period of time there appeared a fully evolved type of Parish Hadley (as the firm became known) room. Specially hand-quilted materials were used as furniture upholstery and pillows. Floors were painted in increasingly elaborate designs. Pattern and color were mixed in the extreme degree that only Mrs. Parish can handle. The traditional designs of New York upholsterers, most of which, although based on old ones, had been modernized over the years, were returned to their earlier, puffier forms. A new look of sybaritic comfort came into existence.

Meanwhile, the glamour of Mrs. Parish's reputation grew as she began to be known for her work for some of the chicest people in the country.

Mr. and Mrs. William Paley (she was, of course, Mrs. Whitney's sister) hired Mrs. Parish to work on their Fifth Avenue apartment and their house in New Hampshire. Over the years, the Paleys had used Syrie Maugham, George Stacey, Billy Baldwin, Natalie Davenport of McMillen, and finally Jansen to help them decorate their houses. Although it sounds preposterously neurotic to run through such a long list of decorators, it was really just a manifestation of a great love of decorating. And, at the time, i.e., the late sixties, the Paleys still had more or less intact rooms by all of those decorators. That's a chapter in itself, though. Then Mrs. Paley's daughter Amanda and her husband,

This view of Mrs. Astor's drawing room is filled with some of the pieces that are typical of the late Freddy Victoria's taste for fancifully unconventional French furniture. A profusion of flowers from the greenhouse adds a deliciously Edwardian touch.

Carter Burden, hired Mrs. Parish and Albert to do their new River House apartment. They decorated a mammoth old shingled house in Maine for Mr. and Mrs. Samuel Reed, a townhouse in New York for Mr. and Mrs. David Rockefeller, houses in Virginia and Washington for Connie Mellon, as well as a penthouse on Park Avenue, and most luxurious of all, a house in San Francisco for Mr. and Mrs. Gordon Getty.

Over the years Mrs. Parish's style has become richer and richer. She has an unabashed love of spaces filled to overflowing. There is a superb confidence about her and her styles. One theory, espoused by a contemporary, attributes this confidence to the combined good fortune of a distinguished family with plenty of money, three adoring brothers (hence the nickname Sister), and of course her unmistakable taste.

As far as influence is concerned, the Sister Parish style has had a continued effect on decorating and decorators for the past twenty-five years. Consider, first of all, the people who have worked for her. When he first came to New York, Keith Irvine worked for her briefly. In the sixties there were Edward Cave, Bill Hodgins, David Easton, Robert Moore, Kevin McNamara, and Bunny Williams, who stayed for twenty years. Harold Simmons was the head of the Parish Hadley design department for many years. More recently, Tice Alexander, David Kleinberg, and Gary Hager have all been associated with the firm. And the partners of the architectural firm Ferguson Murray began there. Mario Buatta's great influences were John Fowler and Mrs. Parish. All through the sixties and seventies, as the English country-house style (so called) gained in popularity here, it was Mrs. Parish who continually kept her American public supplied with her particular interpretation of the increasingly lush trends that seemed to originate on Brook Street, Bond Street, and the Pimlico Road.

The Getty house in San Francisco illustrates the height of the Parish-Hadley style. It is more elaborate, more ornate, than any other expression of Mrs. Parish's taste, and it is appropriate, after all, for the people who live there. The Italianate architecture exactly suits the decoration. The general impression the house makes is one of completely cheerful yet rich luxury. The entrance hall is narrow, with a closed staircase off to the side. Almost immediately after you enter, you come upon the library to the left, its neo-Jacobean paneling painted what is almost a peacock blue. Chintz curtains and valances in a brilliant red, green, and blue design of leaves continue the vibrant tone of the room. Powerful Regency furniture and an Anglo-Indian ivory mirror create an exotic mood that continues in the colonnaded courtyard two stories high in the center of the house. Across the back, the predominantly yellow and gold drawing room and the dining room with antique Chinese wallpaper, a huge Swedish chandelier, and green and gold woodwork form a backdrop for tons of gold leaf, lacquer, and silk in pale colors. If there are any more palatial Georgian chairs to be found than the ones in the Getty drawing room, I haven't seen them. The yellow silk curtains are embellished with huge bows. With all this splendor, however, the atmosphere is festive rather than ponderously formal.

I think it could be said that Mrs. Parish's rooms are usually very cheerful. The voluptuous feminine quality that pervades her work prevents it from being overly serious. And there is usually a strong promise of "creature comfort" that outweighs any possibility of stiff formality. If Mrs. Parish dislikes too much informality, she is still never pompous. Her scathing sense of humor is the antithesis of pomposity. Yet her great aim has always been to convey a feeling of upper-class permanence, whether rich and grand or old-fashioned and nostalgic. And there is always an avoidance of having things look too studied. I remember two examples of this approach that caused Albert great grief. One occurred many years ago when they were finishing a triplex on Park Avenue for Mr. and Mrs. Edgar Bronfman. Between the windows in the master bedroom Mrs. Parish insisted on placing a commode that was slightly too big for the space and that, in consequence, pushed into the curtains on either side. "It looks like they had it and just put it there," said Mrs. Parish in defense of her arrangement. Albert remained unconvinced. The second instance also involved a commode, this one in the drawing room of the apartment of Connie Mellon's that is now owned by the Agnellis. Over the commode hung a beautiful Renoir which was partially obscured by the shade of the lamp on the commode. To solve the problem, Mrs. Parish simply moved the picture off center, another example of her free hand with the placement of furniture and artworks. Again, Albert disagreed with her solution. Their differences (and they are great) notwithstanding, both Mrs. Parish and Albert view decorating with an underlying sense of romance and glamour. Mrs. Parish pretends that it all just happens. Albert pretends that it is highly scientific. In fact, they both practice their craft in the most mysteriously individualistic way possible. That rarest of qualities, originality, instills their work with fresh surprises year after year. The engaging comfort and beauty that they insist upon makes their rooms seem to be free of all the boring rhetoric that can kill a style. Their style is based on deeply personal talent. It's reassuring that so many people recognize the value of that quality and try to imitate it.

Albert Hadley

ALBERT HADLEY WAS BORN IN 1920 IN NASH-
ville, Tennessee. Like most great decorators, his
love of houses was consuming. As a little boy he
threatened to run away from home unless his parents changed the driveway, which he hated, to a circle in front
of the house. This early critical power has only increased over
the years. More than most people, he absorbed what he saw, in
person and through photographs, an ability that has equipped
him with an amazingly detailed memory of what has occurred
in the last half century of decorating. His encyclopedic knowledge extends to all phases of decoration and architecture, as well
as to the personal style of those luminaries who have influenced
taste over the years.

   While still young, he admired the shop in Nashville which
belonged to A. Herbert Rogers. There, the daydream was of

*Albert Hadley's silver living
room in the seventies was
furnished with a collection of
pieces each from a different
place and a different period.
Somehow it was totally
peaceful and serene.*

France, with mansard roofs, arched windows, and parquet de Versailles floors, all added on to a house in Tennessee. Rogers, who had his own workrooms, gave Albert his first job and it was there that Albert became immersed in the total aspect of decoration, from the design to the careful working out of the details to the completion and installation of the job. All of these phases he mastered and to this day he works directly with the people who make the curtains and the furniture and the paint samples, with a complete knowledge of what they are faced with in producing the demanding elements of interior decoration. Albert, far more than many of his colleagues, can operate profitably with pins, scissors, and muslin, and he is able to explain how curtains should hang, how valances should be draped, and how upholstered furniture, spoiled over the years by modernizing changes, should be redesigned from traditional models. His insistence on trying out new details has had a huge influence on the New York upholstery trade. Sometimes the new details are in fact old ones. Nevertheless, trying out new ways of presenting the finished product has given Parish-Hadley upholstered furniture a distinctive appearance, softer and more luxurious than is traditional, with a look apparent only in hand-made pieces. These aspects have influenced decorators all over the country for the last twenty-five years.

Albert's early idols were Elsie de Wolfe, Ruby Ross Wood, George Stacey, and Dorothy Draper, all of whom, except Elsie de Wolfe, were at the height of their careers in the forties, when Albert arrived in New York. Another idol of Albert's, who had a profound influence on his unorthodox way of viewing things, was William Pahlmann, whose designs were known for their extraordinary daring. Pahlmann's lack of interest in historical dogma appealed to Albert's love of the unexpected. There's a distinct paradox in the Albert Hadley point of view: on the one hand, he dotes on the romantic past; on the other, he searches continuously for original effects more in tune with the present day.

Cecil Beaton was another figure whose writings and drawings Albert devoured. Beaton produced so many diaries and scrapbooks that any serious daydreamer hoping one day to be a decorator would have had to spend masses of time consulting them. Albert's prodigious memory seems to have absorbed them all.

During the Second World War Albert was in the Army, stationed in England. Afterward, he returned to the United States and in 1946 came to New York to stay. George Stacey, one of his idols and one of the most successful New York decorators of the time, recommended that he go to see Mrs. Archibald Brown at McMillen. Mrs. Brown, wearing a neat little veil wrapped around her head, lectured Albert on the importance of studying at the Parsons School. Following her advice, he began his course there in 1947. It was in a Parsons classroom in Long Island City that Albert first encountered Van Day Truex, who was dressed as usual with impeccable flair in a sienna-colored tweed suit, with one sleeve cuff turned down, one turned up. The Truex style, with its complex mixture of classicism, modernism, and unpretentious simplicity, had an immediate effect on Albert. While he was at Parsons, he excelled to the extent that he was given a scholarship to the Paris branch of the school, which unfortunately he was unable to use. Finally, however, he was asked to join the faculty, which initiated his teaching career. For five years he taught Parsons students, and his great gift for teaching has never left him. He is unsurpassed in his ability to train others, whether they are his clients or his assistants.

In 1957, Albert went to work for Mrs. Brown and for the next four years he collaborated with the august ladies of McMillen, Inc. During that period he worked, among other things, on a restoration of Rosedown Plantation in Louisiana. With its beautiful Victorian furniture, Rosedown evoked Albert's Southern devotion to antebellum decoration. At Tiffany he once created a luncheon setting using a charming Victorian sofa and painted and gilded Victorian tables and chairs, all of this at a time when Victorian taste was rather frowned upon. For Mr. and Mrs. Joshua Logan, in their River House apartment, Albert helped to create a daring and very romantic atmosphere reminiscent of the Paris of Louis Philippe, with Brussels-weave patterned carpets bought by the Logans at Madeleine Castaing's Paris shop, swagged curtains heavily fringed, lace undercurtains, and Victorian upholstered pieces recalling scenes by Berthe Morisot or Edgar Degas—Degas being particularly appropriate since there were several pictures by him on the deep red walls of that dense and moody room. This style of decorating has since become very popular and is now often seen, but when Albert created this enchanting essay on Victoriana for the Logans, it was new and original. Before the room was installed, the Logans appeared unexpectedly in the midst of the glazing of the red walls. Their reaction was violent and negative. "But wait," Albert pleaded, "this is not opening night yet. You have to see it finished." Charmed by the show-business argument, they relented, and they adored their drawing room forever after. It was a fantasy of the nineteenth century, rather than a curatorial recreation. In the back of Albert's mind is always the idea of

Shaped valances like those in a Venetian palace, loose covers like the ones you see in Victorian paintings, and a pastel color scheme give this room a playful twist typical of Albert's work. The black candles are a reminder of Rose Cumming.

fantasy; even in his most serious work, this playful aesthetic is never ignored. It can be said that he is serious about being playful. He has always had a fascination with Florine Stettheimer, the artist, aesthete, and scenic designer whose salon throughout the thirties and forties was unique in New York for its appeal to artists and writers. One of the rooms cited by Albert as a decorating achievement he wishes he could have seen is Miss Stettheimer's legendary studio apartment, with its cellophane curtains, white-painted furniture, and seashell flowers everywhere.

Albert's love of fantasy operates on two levels: the fantasy object itself, and also the people in the past to whom these rooms of fantasy and their objects refer. If Albert's white-painted palm-tree torchères were marvelous in their own right, their appeal to him was even greater because they were designed by Emilio Terry and had belonged to Elsie Mendl. The same is true for the white plaster dolphin table made by Syrie Maugham, which for years stood in Albert's drawing room.

When I first met Albert in 1963, his apartment was filled with furniture of a delicate but still substantial design quality: the palm-tree torchères, the dolphin table, white-painted Louis XVI-style chairs probably from northern Italy. There was a chandelier of red Venetian glass, and the coffee table, made in the twenties, was of red mirror with gold edges. On the floor were black and white cowhide rugs. The color scheme was white, ice blue, and deep ruby red, a scheme that might have been devised in the twenties or thirties by Ruby Ross Wood or by Mrs. Maugham herself. Although Albert's subsequent apartments and weekend houses have been decorated primarily in shades of beige and white, his fondness for pale blue accented with red has continued. A few years ago he painted a large drawing room in an old Southampton shingled house the cold, pale blue he loves and covered nearly all the furniture in red and white cotton. Red glass and old pieces of needlework containing shades of red recalled to me his own room of thirty years ago.

In 1962, Albert left McMillen to go to work for Mrs. Henry Parish II. By 1963 he was in full swing, soon to become her partner. The name of the firm was eventually changed to Parish-Hadley.

Along with his love of atmospheric decoration tinged with fantasy, Albert possesses a remarkable ability to tackle the architectural problems of the houses and apartments he is working on. To a large extent, this ability was informed and refined by the years he spent working at McMillen, where the drafting department was under the eagle eye of the brilliant Grace Fakes, an excellent designer-decorator, who, after distinguished decorating work on her own, joined the firm of McMillen and became one of Mrs. Brown's staunchest employees in the work that has been carried on there for so many decades. With the experience Albert had gained, he was able with Mrs. Parish to expand their work into an increasing area of architecture and decoration, giving the firm a stronger imprint than it had in the past. Albert's talent, joined with Mrs. Parish's own point of view, enabled them to become, during the sixties and seventies, the most talked-about and exciting decorating firm in the United States. Eventually Parish-Hadley developed, under Albert's direction, an architectural department capable of executing work on a very large scale. This capability occurred at a time when the old-fashioned architects of New York, who had been so involved with the

Thirty years ago, Albert's studio apartment was a blue and white backdrop for his collection of Elsie de Wolfe and Syrie Maugham white plaster pieces. The chandelier and mirrored coffee table were made of red glass.

decorating projects of previous decades, were disappearing completely. Mott Schmidt died in 1977, and Page Cross in 1975, to name two celebrated examples. It became increasingly important for Albert to take on remodeling and redesigning projects of greater scope. He constantly sought new design solutions and looked ahead to fresh ideas, which created trends soon followed by others in the field. The elaborate paintwork associated with the Parish-Hadley firm was extremely influential twenty years ago and has had a lasting effect on decorators throughout the United States: walls striéed in two directions, giving the impression of plaid; dark colors sanded and varnished to a mirrorlike gloss; floors stenciled and incised in all kinds of patterns. These trademarks of Albert's love of elaborately refined finishes appeared in the work of all the Parish-Hadley followers, of whom there are many. With him in this enterprise, of course, was Mrs. Parish, whose own ideas of decorating were equally spirited. It is fair to say that Mrs. Parish and Albert have a stimulating effect on each other that has enabled them as partners to achieve a body of exciting work that would have been difficult for either to accomplish on his or her own. The work they did together for a number of tremendously stylish clients—Annette and Samuel Reed, the Paleys, who seemed to explore the possibilities of redecorating on a virtually continuous basis, Louise and Freddy Melhado (to name a few)—combined their differing viewpoints in a fresh, inventive way.

While Mrs. Parish's well-known love of chintz and old-fashioned country details, a combination of her passion for her summer rural life in Maine and the quirky luxury of English houses, was the major inspiration of her work, Albert has traditionally had a more eccentric and individualistic approach. He has always separated the roles of architecture and decoration in designing a room. His sense of architecture is cool and disciplined, but his preferences in decoration have always been for the unconventional and the unexpected. He has a gift for blending a classical and an anticlassical approach. I have always felt that Albert would like his clients, once the job is done, to feel that they were highly original aesthetes living in an atmosphere unlike anybody else's. It is this desire for individuality, achieved through a combination of classic design and the unique aspects of collecting, that has always driven Albert in his pursuit of rooms that are noteworthy for their lack of formula.

The wide range of influences on Albert Hadley's taste, which includes William Pahlmann, Jean-Michel Frank, Van Day Truex, in addition to the more romantic figures from the past, like Elsie Mendl and Syrie Maugham, has given his work a rich variety of styles and references. Since joining Mrs. Parish nearly thirty years ago, Albert has continued to expand this varied roster of influence by his interest in the English decorating that fascinated Mrs. Parish: the style pioneered by Nancy Lancaster and John Fowler during their partnership at the London firm of Colefax & Fowler. John Fowler was part of an era in England, beginning in the early twentieth century, of decorators, professional and amateur, who loved the unexpected touch in the decoration of houses—old elements worked in with new ones in ways that stressed the long evolution of decoration within a house. John Fowler was never a modernist in the way that Albert can be, but there is in the work of both men a reverence for the unconventional touch which can give an element of surprise to a room. In lavish decorating, that surprise often consists of a detail that is disarmingly simple. During our present era of increasingly rich Edwardian taste, Albert has never lost his desire for sleekness and simplicity. Sometimes this means the introduction of something distinctly modern. Occasionally it is expressed by the use of rustic furniture and objects that reveal Albert's love of arts and crafts and his abhorrence of excessive richness. An example of this is a large, two-story room he decorated in Chicago years ago that combined all of the eclectic

Long before most designers were pondering the twenties and thirties, Albert was immersed in a study of those glamorous decades. He created this staircase thirty years ago.

elements of Albert's American mixture of styles. It had rough bamboo blinds, painted materials by Alan Campbell (a craftsman whose work was largely discovered by Albert and Mrs. Parish), and furniture of a broadly diverse nature. The tables alone illustrated this free hand: there was one made of chrome and glass, one skirted in yellow silk, a Moroccan one inlaid with mother of pearl, a Louis XIII oak center table, and a lacquered Chinese-style coffee table. An enormous tin chandelier occupied the sleek upper space of this almost Bauhaus-like plaster shell. It was a room of the present, filled with objects from the past.

The "chic of suitability" is often quoted by Albert as his motto. What he finds unsuitable is overdecoration that is neither appropriate for the twentieth century nor forward-looking or comfortable enough to be realistic for people of our time. Albert's fascination with who and what is chic has enabled him to work brilliantly with some of the most stylish people of his time. Unlike most decorators, who work in a rigid style that can always be identified as their own, Albert seeks ways to express the taste of the people whose houses he decorates.

A number of years ago Albert redesigned the library in Mrs. Vincent Astor's Park Avenue apartment. Seeing it for the first time, Van Day Truex said that he considered it the best new room he'd seen in New York "in many, many years." The bookcases, which are all edged in brass, an echo perhaps of the brass bookcases Billy Baldwin designed for Cole Porter's Waldorf Tower apartment some twenty years earlier, are filled with the beautiful polished bindings of Mrs. Astor's books. Van said that it was like looking into a room lined in Coromandel lacquer. The walls of this lovely library are glazed a rich sang-de-boeuf red color and have been repeatedly varnished, so that they sparkle almost as brightly as the brass strips that surround the bookcases themselves. The floor is a highly polished antique parquet de Versailles and the furniture is covered in the La Portugaise chintz brought to New York by Rose Cumming, with its bold brown stripes and multicolored flowers repeating the red of the walls and the colors in the antique Bessarabian carpet on the floor. Then there are French chairs covered in plain reds and off-white. The sleek, modern quality of this room in no way makes it inappropriate for the antique furniture and the old polished bindings and is a perfect background for Mrs. Astor's personality, which is also chic, glamorous, and completely of our time.

In a rigorous way, Albert's own apartments have provided him with a decorating laboratory over the years, enabling him to try out new techniques and materials that have taken his fancy, such as floors stenciled and painted in bold patterns or covered in palm matting; walls lacquered, varnished, or papered with silver tea paper; ceilings painted any number of colors. Albert's tremendous energy goes into continuously experimenting with the ideas that come and go in his constant search for a fresh approach. His furniture arrangements, with increasing and decreasing numbers of pieces, have revealed over the years the inner workings of his mind. Is less more, or is less less? In the 1970s he lived in a beautiful apartment in a handsome townhouse off Fifth Avenue. At first the walls were covered in a brown paper the color of a shopping bag. After that they were covered in silver, antiqued paper of a beautiful smoky quality. The floors were sometimes bare, with small scatterings of carpets on top of whatever finish he would be toying with at the moment. For a time they were covered in palm matting at a moment when straw matting was first seen. The room achieved its greatest beauty when the floors were stenciled in white and a very soft shade of black with white rubbed through. The walls were covered in the silver paper, and the furniture was upholstered very softly in either a linen printed in a dark brown, wood-grain pattern on off-white or in a plain natural color. His collection of white plaster furniture and white-painted Louis XVI chairs was still intact and placed around the room. There was a David Adler pine console table in the style of William Kent, like the console tables at Castle Hill in Ipswich, Massachusetts. It was a room reminiscent of all of Albert's idols: Elsie Mendl, Rose Cumming, Billy Baldwin, Syrie Maugham, and David Adler. But it was, more than that, very much Albert's own.

In his various apartments there have always been cocktail parties at which one would meet any number of people, young and old, involved in the decorating world. More than anyone I've known, Albert has as his friends people who not only share his love of decoration, architecture, and design, but who also work in those fields. And, more than anyone I've known, Albert, throughout his career, has trained people in a patient way that reveals his tremendous gift for teaching. Among those of us who have worked for him are Kevin McNamara, William Hodgins, David Easton, Bunny Williams, Robert Moore, and Harold Simmons. Unlike many of Albert's past and present colleagues, who would prefer to spend their days in French restaurants with their chic clients, Albert would rather be chatting around the fire with a bunch of young people whose passion for the complete scope of decoration and design equals his own. Not that many people can match his scope. The outstanding characteristic of his style, both professionally and personally, is his eternally youthful outlook and whimsical fascination with a kind of movie-star glamour that is shared and understood by all of us who adore decoration for and by those who have possessed great style and chic. How he balances make-believe with reality is not easy to figure out, but it is a fact that he is able to bring to any room a fantastic mixture of elements combining the past and the present better than most people can. Perhaps better than anyone can.

Geoffrey Bennison

OHN FOWLER CREATED A NEW STYLE OF EN-glish decoration which was fully defined by the middle of the 1950s, when he and Nancy Lancaster had worked together for nearly ten years. But by then distinct factions had broken away, becoming branches of new design philosophies that would, during the sixties, shoot off further in several directions. Some of these took fifties modernism to more restrained, classical levels; others chose to dwell on traditional design couched in contemporary terms. Designers in the latter category continued to develop the shock value of unusual juxtapositions, a practice of the fifties certainly. But where a lot of fifties design seemed to be willfully anticlassical, even jarring, the new trend of the sixties was less crazy, paving the way undoubtedly for the emergence of postmodernism, as we call it now.

In a French country drawing room for David and Olympia de Rothschild, Geoffrey Bennison covered the walls in stamped Córdoba leather and freely combined French and English elements in order to achieve his particular brand of lush, moody decor.

A lot was going on in the design world in the sixties. It looks, all these years later, to have been an ephemeral period, one in which thoughts were collected and ideas were run through but only in the spirit of getting ready for something else. One of the people who was certainly getting ready for something else was Geoffrey Bennison (1921–84), a unique figure in the London antiques-dealing milieu and one whose radius of influence continued to lengthen all of his life.

Bennison, who was born in Lancashire, was a brilliant art student at the Slade School, which had moved temporarily to Oxford during World War II. His brilliance was particularly sparkling in the areas of painting and stage design. Circumstances pushed him, however, into the antiques business and then into interior decorating. His father, who died when he was twelve, had been a building contractor; his mother ran a curtain-making concern. And after a terrible period as a young man of fighting tuberculosis and living in sanatoria in England and Switzerland, Geoffrey Bennison, making what must have been a natural decision, began selling antiques and objects in a Bermondsey Market stall, a four-year period he loved. Following that, he had a shop in Islington and finally, for over twenty years, he was an enchanting figure in the Pimlico area, presiding over a shop that captured a mood that was totally romantic. Geoffrey's shop, as did John Fowler's, supplied him with a steady flow of materials with which to work, and as the proprietor shaped the contents of his shop, the contents themselves shaped the emerging style. This incredible shop, with its abundance of exotic stock arranged in an even more exotic, almost Moorish way, was, in fact, the staging ground for the Bennison style, a decorating phase of the future that was in the works.

At Colefax & Fowler the mood was one of offhand, cozy refinement, with furniture and objects of charming prettiness and of course lightness combined in an original way that was at the same time fresh but old-fashioned. At Geoffrey's shop, with its cavelike atmosphere (as though it had been created by a Georgian version of Léon Bakst), one always had the feeling of making discoveries. Of course, they were *Geoffrey's* discoveries. He was continuously making them and passing them along, and while he was engaged in this marvelous search, he was sizing up the design world, keeping an eye on the trends, whether or not they affected his singular vision. Twenty-seven years ago, he wrote a piece for the London *Times* in which he discussed what he considered the three main trends in the antiques business. First, there was what he called "the current oak boom"—medieval, Renaissance, and Louis XIII. Then a new interest in Art Nouveau. Neither of these, he predicted, would last long. His use of the word "slimy" to describe the lines of much of the commonly seen Art Nouveau furniture was typical of his humor.

The third trend he named was one that described his style. He called it "New Trad," and defined it as a lasting trend, not really new, that was, in his words, anti-decoration and pro-"things." "The basic elements are a combination of good English and French furniture of the 18th century with useful furniture of any period and century." Philosophically, there is an enormous freedom in this method of decoration; Geoffrey Bennison's taste, however free, consisted of a broad but identifiable range of preferences, to which was added the inimitable quality of his eye (particularly ironic, since he is so imitated). The foundation of his rooms was often (usually, one might say) a Ziegler carpet, a genre of carpet made in Iran in the nineteenth century for the export market. The colors—brick reds, blues, off-whites, and tans—were ideally suited to two other elements of Geoffrey's decorating vocabulary, namely the large, softly colored Imari jars, also with their reds and blues, and his "Red Riding Hood" red, a paint color which is, in his friend John Richardson's words, a hard-to-achieve dull scarlet. To this, I might add that it is also one of the most interestingly neutral (we all know what boringly neutral means) background colors, welcoming the combined use of other reds, blues, greens, browns, yellows. Geoffrey could even make mauvey tones work with it. His rooms were full of sculpture: bronze, marble, and plaster casts. Great busts on pedestals were particularly loved and contributed to the impression of centuries of collections or ancestors or something from the heroic past. The tops of gigantic bookcases and cabinets were loaded with perfectly arranged groups of heads and figures or vases in the spirit of Daniel Marot. Upholstered pieces in their original leather or velvet melted into the rest of the old materials he loved—tapestry, crewel, and faded patterns of all sorts. There was an overall sense of largeness, huge-scale mirrors and cupboards, especially in the style of William Kent. Geoffrey's shop was the constant expression of this consistently evolving taste, and decorators and dealers found it necessary to keep a very close eye on what was coming and going through the doors. The Bennison style appealed to a wide range of tastes. John Fowler admired the shop, as did Tom Parr, who joined Colefax & Fowler in 1960. David Hicks and Christopher Gibbs were regulars, as were Robert Denning and Vincent Fourcade. His appeal was enormous and unpredictable. So, of course, was his knowledge, aided always by his miraculous eye.

Geoffrey's own London sitting room was a balanced synthesis of brilliant collecting and bookish comfort, a perfect reflection of its owner's taste and personality.

Geoffrey was alert to everything about the decorating world. His eyes, bright and constantly moving from place to place, object to object, were a clear sign of his restless fascination with the things around him, and he obviously could absorb anything he wanted to in the broad field of interior decoration. Twenty or so years ago he decorated a library in London for the publisher George Weidenfeld, in which there were references backward and forward, taking in the past and present in a way that only those who adore the complete topic of design can do. Billy Baldwin's library for Cole Porter was evoked by brass bookcases and shiny brown walls. Geoffrey even used the brass swing-arm lamps that Billy loved all around the room. A geometrically patterned carpet covered the floor, the way miles of similar carpets were covering floors all over at the time. A Francis Bacon hung over the fireplace. The only thing in the room that seemed typical of Geoffrey's taste was a large nineteenth-century library table with scrolled legs. On this table stood a typical Bennison bust. In the other rooms of the flat there were traces characteristic of the classic Bennison taste; it was, however, an example of design executed in the style of the time by one who is associated with an entirely different point of view. His true style, that complex moodiness achieved by a romantic mixture of cozy Victoriana and muscular, classical ornamentation on a grand scale, became widely known to a new public through a pivotal phase of his career, when he became the decorator in charge of a number of projects for the Rothschilds.

Just as *le style Rothschild* caught the fancy of Second Empire France a hundred years before, Geoffrey's version of that venerable expression of luxury set in motion a new decorating mania—*his* Rothschild style. For David Rothschild and his wife he first decorated in Paris a stupendous apartment that contains a phenomenal Louis XIV enfilade, the rooms of which are grand, palatial, and historic—qualities that might make one a little nervous. Not Geoffrey. Like a sorcerer, he conjured up a spell that takes you through many eras, but not at all in a nervous way. The combination of great architecture and sympathetic taste prevented any confusion, yet the mixtures are remarkable. The hall at the top of the stairs firmly establishes a mood of drama and beauty that prepares you for what you might expect, provided you can keep up. This fabulous hall, with its typical tan and white marble floor, has walls heavily draped and fringed in pink, a device that was used by Geoffrey to cover pale blue scagliola that he didn't find sympathetic but that he was unable to refinish because of the preservation rules and restrictions that governed a great deal of the historic decoration of these rooms. In fact, his admonishment—"no cherubs, dear"—had to be overlooked in this instance owing to the existence of pairs of putti over each of the four doors, supporting plaster drapery that dissolves into the folds of the real material hung around the room. On the wall opposite as you enter hangs an enormous equestrian portrait flanked by tall marble columns supporting porphyry urns. The composition of this painting and its attending columns and urns recalls the major sense of scale and decoration that enabled Charles de Beistegui to create his unforgettable rooms of almost forty years before. The painting, one of a pair, came from Beistegui's Palazzo Labia in Venice, a house to which Geoffrey attributed a renewed interest in Louis XIII furniture. Like ghosts from the past (ghosts we all wish we could know), spirits from centuries on end fill these rooms, in a way so convincing that it is impossible to tell what was recently purchased from what has been collected by generations of family. Roman marble busts on pedestals (there are four in all in the hall),

Guy de Rothschild's New York bedroom illustrated Geoffrey Bennison's unparalleled ability to pile patterns of all sorts on top of one another.

seventeenth-, eighteenth-, and nineteenth-century furniture ranging from royal-looking pieces by Cressent to velour- and turkey-carpet-covered extravagances of the Victorian upholsterer's runaway imagination—all of these stand side by side in completely poised comfort, and of course they assure you that they *are* comfortable. There is none of that ghastly attitude of staggering investment value that attaches itself to those rooms where collecting seems a business, not a passion.

ERRATUM

The publisher regrets that there is an error on page 238 of this edition.
Depicted here is the correct illustration of Geoffrey Bennison's design for
Guy de Rothschild's New York bedroom.

In the rooms continuing off the hall—a study, a sitting room, and a dining room—Geoffrey combined fabulous Rothschild possessions spanning ten different periods with his own strong and skillful designs—bookcases inspired by Sir John Soane, cupboards appropriately recalling Paxton and Lami at Ferrières, the great nineteenth-century Rothschild château (these cupboards are appropriately filled with gold plate and oriental porcelain), and porcelain-laden overmantels that could be straight out of a painting by François Desportes. The Bennison signature is everywhere, woven into the owners' own: the deep, moody colors, the Persian carpets, complicated Victorian chairs upholstered in velour and tapestry with heavy fringe, crewel curtains, green pleated lampshades, and row after row of porcelain vases.

After this marvelous decorating project, Geoffrey redesigned the rooms of the château near Deauville that also belongs to the Rothschilds, leaving some of the curtains and walls as they were and transforming others— as in the case of the drawing room, which is now hung in embossed leather that Geoffrey found and restored. Much simpler than the flat in Paris, these rooms express the exact note of country ease that you would imagine wanting to have as a contrast to a very grand house in town; the elements that preoccupied Geoffrey in his work, however, are all there.

Then, in another vein, but combining related furniture and objects belonging to the same family, Geoffrey decorated an apartment in New York for David Rothschild's parents, Baron and Baroness Guy de Rothschild, in a building designed by Charles Adams Platt and built in 1907. The apartment contains, on two floors, cozy, houselike rooms arranged around a great central room twenty feet high. With its beamed ceiling and stone chimney, this cubelike room, painted and stenciled by Geoffrey and filled with furniture and porcelain stored away after Ferrières had passed out of the Rothschilds' hands, is a unique recreation of the most romantic nineteenth-century love of the Renaissance one can imagine. Because it was decorated in a taste we can not only understand but also admire, it is not marred by that ersatz quality of phony accuracy that makes most turn-of-the-century Renaissance interiors look like model rooms in a museum. Instead, the decoration here achieves that most difficult of all fantasies: it looks as though these rooms were a hundred and twenty years old.

As you cross the somber little stair hall, filled with engravings and pictures that disappear up the narrow stairs, and enter the twenty-foot-tall drawing room, your first impression is of the great height, which comes as a big surprise after the small entrance hall. The next impression is of the pleasing gloom (the room faces an interior courtyard), and immediately upon registering the gloom, you become aware of the tall, extraordinary lace curtains through which the pale north daylight travels, illuminating, with the help of the Bennison porcelain lamps and the brass chandelier, a treasure house of rich and heroic objects—marble busts of Roman emperors, marquetry and pietra dura cabinets, bronze doré, ebony, and Boulle pieces. Italian majolica jars stand in rows on shelves built into the overdoors. Plates and dishes of the same earthenware hang on the walls. Likewise, the tufted and fringed chairs and sofas possess the properties of antiquity that link all the other elements of the room. The stenciled wainscoting and the Turkish carpet appear

The corner of his London sitting room where the table for dining was placed had as its dominant center point one of Geoffrey's typical "Wunder Kammer" arrangements of sculpture, shells, coral, and so on. The painting of the domed villa is Russian.

to have come into existence at the same time; nothing about the room reveals its recent birth. Best of all, it belongs to the Rothschilds and is therefore entirely appropriate, filled as it is with generations of *their* possessions, many of which came from Ferrières. A small library with skillfully lit books and an equally small dining room with nineteenth-century Indian crewelwork panels fastened to the walls with huge metal nails complete this suite of perfectly patterned and textured rooms. If it sounds as though this is all more to do with decorating than collecting, I should point out that paintings by Rembrandt, Goya, and Ingres, to name just a few of the artists represented, hang alongside the nineteenth-century family portraits.

Geoffrey's own apartment, newly decorated and moved into a few years before his death, felt more like a cottage in the country than a flat in London—architecturally, that is, because Geoffrey's presence implied its own geography. The spaces were not Georgian and they were not Victorian. They were low and horizontal. Others would have gotten busy with a lot of cornice moldings, but not Geoffrey, who realized that they would do no good. Instead, working with his own palette, his own materials (colored as though the dying vats were filled with tea), and his mammoth collection of books, pictures, furniture, and objects, he created rooms arranged with a dense deftness that transcended the architectureless character of the place. Generous down-filled sofas, a desk, and a high Flemish cupboard, all of which would more typically have been found in a bigger, taller room, defined areas for sitting, writing, and eating. Deep window reveals, created by floor-to-ceiling bookcases, gave the walls the depth and weight that old buildings usually possess. On the remaining walls, pictures of every imaginable scale were hung in intricately patterned arrangements. The background, naturally, was Red Riding Hood red.

What Geoffrey achieved in his exquisitely moody rooms was a romantically beautiful expression of nostalgia and comfort. The Victorian past he evoked has been purged of all the un-gainliness that was often there. The graceful humor that made Geoffrey's presence so enchanting, his fey playfulness, his in-capacity to be pompous, not to mention his formidable taste and connoisseurship, allowed him to venture into realms of weighty grandeur without ever straying into that awful, rich people's world of "no fun" seriousness. Like some Proustian arbiter of taste and manners, he knew exactly how to get it right, while at the same time he left a tingling impression of mystery. How did he do it? Where did it all come from? The decorator magician. That's what he was.

Madeleine Castaing

*O*NE OF THE GREAT UNRESOLVED DEBATES IN interior decorating is whose taste should be evident in the finished work. Should it be the decorator's? Or should it be the client's? There are those designers whose forte is the interpretation of the personal style of the connoisseur or the tastemaker. Their best efforts are frequently identified with the exciting personalities for whom they work. With the ability (and the willingness) to subordinate their own preferences to the wishes of their dominating clients, decorators of this category can achieve a great variety of styles.

On the other hand, there are those very noticeable but rare designers whose originality and single-mindedness enable them to devise an individual style of decorating that belongs to them alone. Sometimes, of course, decorating of this nature becomes monotonous. But once in a while there comes along a figure in

In spite of the passage of time, Mme. Castaing's rooms in Paris are sharp and crisp, focusing on the individual style of each piece, yet possessing a totally integrated style that is completely hers.

245

the design world who stands alone, isolated, fascinating, and charged with the power to influence others while still defying easy imitation. It is interesting that two of this century's most compelling design originals are French. One was Jean-Michel Frank. The other is Madeleine Castaing. Frank was a modernist whose creations relied on the inspiration of the past, restating the grand proportions and classical discipline of French architecture and design, but in a minimalist, twentieth-century fashion. Madeleine Castaing, however, is not a modernist. Hers is the style of an invented past. In the words of the editors of *The World of Interiors*, "Her work has the quality of rooms remembered from dreams, or imagined while reading novels. Hers is the taste of retrospection." Not surprisingly, Madame Castaing herself says that she has probably learned Proust by heart, so often has she read him (twelve times). All of this hints at the complexity of her style, a style that has progressed in its purity through more than four decades.

Madeleine Castaing was born in 1894 in Chartres. At the age of eighteen, she married Marcellin Castaing, an art critic and businessman who was a friend and admirer of Modigliani. Through him, and with much difficulty and perseverance, the Castaings came to know the reclusive and eccentric painter Soutine. For a while, Soutine lived in the Castaing country house, and when he died in 1943, Madame Castaing inherited the bulk of his estate. By then, she had become an arresting figure in the world of French interior decoration. The Castaings restored their house outside Chartres, which Madeleine had known since childhood, to an imaginary moment of the Directoire period, when it had been built. But, as in all of Madame Castaing's work, historicity was not her aim. The creation of period rooms has

Her country drawing room contains all of the apparatus of the Madeleine Castaing style. The architecture, colors, leopard carpet, eccentric furniture—even the turquoise lampshades—everything bears her stamp.

never concerned her. She simply made up a style that encompassed all of her favorite things, including the moods captured in the writings of Stendhal and Balzac.

From the end of the war years on, Madame Castaing has been known for her shop in Paris on the corner of Rue Jacob and Rue Bonaparte. Her flat upstairs is a continuing monument to her taste, as is the shop, with its spaces decorated like the

The mood of this striped and tented entrance hall with its mille fleurs *carpet falls somewhere between a military tent and a room in a Russian novel.*

rooms in a house, an idea she pioneered almost sixty years ago. The extraordinary continuity of her taste is something of a marvel. Certainly it represents an unwavering dedication on her part.

As one might guess, Madame Castaing does not suffer from vagueness. Her thoughts on her career are sharp and clear. Although she has two sons, she nevertheless states flatly that, for a woman to succeed on a creative level, she must negate her maternal instincts. In another provocative sentence, Madame Castaing has said that the reason women don't have it all is that they don't want it. This is not a woman shy about expressing herself. Her decorating is equally decisive.

Although the style of Madame Castaing is tremendously original, it fits into some of the currents of French decoration of the thirties, especially the cool, classical designs of Emilio Terry, the Paris architect of Cuban descent whose work throughout the thirties and forties set a standard of neoclassical revivalism unequaled since. His idols were Palladio and Ledoux, but he dreamed in a palatial mood. The cold classicism of Ledoux echoes throughout the *premiers étages* of Madame Castaing's houses as well. Grandeur and pomposity do not enter in, though. And superimposed over the cool plasterwork and numerous arches she loves, one often finds (and this is her romantic invention) an airy, mid-nineteenth-century layer of decoration, as though a later style has been carefully preserved along with the original architectural background of an earlier period.

The architecture of these rooms means everything. It endows them with their reality. On top of that reality lie the layers of fantasy produced by the imagination of Madame Castaing. The ingredients, varied though they are, have not changed for many years. First of all, her palette is instantly recognizable— cool greens, from a dark, bottle green often used for carpets to a pale, mint-colored shade for walls. Moldings in flat white heighten the crisp coolness of these backgrounds. Clear blues— turquoise, sky blue, and a deep ultramarine—all of which combine well with green are frequently used as bright accents, or as the basis of predominantly blue and white schemes. In bedrooms and dressing rooms a chaste, little-girl pink is often added to the blue or the green motif, or all three colors are used together. An alternative neutral grey, cool like the other shades, is sometimes substituted for white or combined with it.

The lamps in a Madeleine Castaing room are another unmistakable trademark, chiefly because of their steeply slanted paper shades, usually shiny black or green. These lamps are liable to be opaline glass (which comes in her favorite colors) oil lamps that have been converted to electricity. There are no Chinese porcelain lamps in her rooms; in fact, she has never used Chinese porcelains in her decorating. Nor are there any oriental carpets. Madame Castaing uses carpets in designs she invented or revived from nineteenth-century patterns. Like practically everything else in her rooms, the carpet is a trademark. Woven in narrow strips to be sewn together and usually with a cut pile, her carpets range from a couple of different paisleys in two colors, one being black, to the dense, tiny leaves and flowers on dark grounds to the slightly wobbly geometric patterns that have stripes of color running through them. Then, as a counterpoint to the colors of these carpets, she has always used tawny, natural-colored ones, woven in animal patterns, primarily leopard spots, allowing the occasional beige tone (she dislikes beige) to enter into her rather exclusive color range.

The Castaing lexicon of favored materials is equally exclusive: stripes of all kinds, borders used as edgings and applied as stripes, bamboo designs printed on cotton, and a number of odd floral patterns with palm fronds and banana leaves often used as window shades. For bedrooms, she has relied on a mélange of candy-cane stripes, small-scale flower prints of an extremely feminine nature, and starched organdy, all floating on some dark, forestial carpet of her design.

While the structural side of Madeleine Castaing's rooms has always been organized along exceptionally strict lines, the furniture and objects that have caught her fancy over the years are much more diverse. During exactly the same period that Jansen and the other grand decorators of Paris were lavishing on their rooms ormolu-mounted commodes, Aubusson carpets, and signed giltwood chairs, Madame Castaing was cornering the market on severe mahogany furniture from the very late eighteenth century on—the more eccentric, the better. She included, a novelty in France, English Regency pieces. In a 1953 *House & Garden* photograph of one of her bedrooms, there is even an American four-poster bed, lacquered black and draped with organdy and cotton tassels. The color scheme of that room was grey, pink, and black. Many of her pieces—bookcases, tables, torchères—are decorated with arrows and spears, which lend them a lightly military quality, a quality seen in all of the striped, tented rooms she created again and again. Memories of Rome and Napoleon. With this rigidly neoclassical furniture, she mixes, in a deliciously capricious mood, all the tufting, gilded-rope twists and bamboo turnings and wacky shapes of Second Empire upholstery and the designs of Fournier. She then pushes further into the late nineteenth century and the designs of Thonet. Interspersed amid this wide range of styles is often furniture from the period of Charles X, frequently with a Gothic motif, as well as pieces from Russia. Her rooms bore the stamp of Russian, Baltic, and Biedermeier styles long before most other decorators were giving them a thought. There is certainly a cool, northern quality to a great deal of her work. None of the hot fuss and bother that is so adored at the present time weighs down her coolly imaginative rooms.

Forty years later, the starched, gauzy quality of this bedroom in Madeleine Castaing's house has the fresh clarity that distinguishes all of her work.

The influence that emanated from her shop, before and after the war, spread all over France and beyond. One of her greatest friends and constant visitors was Louise de Vilmorin. In America, Billy Baldwin and Natalie Davenport at McMillen, two decorators whose sights were always focused on Paris, not London, schemed the Castaing carpets and materials into many of their rooms. For eighteen years I have worked at keeping one of Billy's beautiful evocations of the Castaing style intact, even moving a thirty-year-old black and green paisley carpet from its original Fifth Avenue home to its new location on Park Avenue. In this new room, the walls are upholstered, once again, in the green and blue, huge-scale tree-of-life pattern used so often by

Madame Castaing. Bamboo tables and blue and white striped curtains continue the recollection of her style.

In the stair hall of an Edwardian house on Long Island, Natalie Davenport, some twenty-five years ago, captured the Proustian mood Madame Castaing translated so effectively by using her black carpet densely covered with leaves, flowers, and berries, combined with antique paisley, Victorian objects, and enormous potted palms. The appearance of Odette Swann at any moment would have been no surprise.

Given the strong sense of line, of sharp silhouette, that the rooms of Madeleine Castaing possess and the consistent repetition that she has always practiced, it is not difficult to understand the distinctive memory her work leaves behind. Yet, in some miraculous way, she has escaped the curse of monotony. Year after year, as she is "discovered" by one young decorator after another, it is made clear all over again what originality and vision she represents. Russian, Biedermeier, Napoleon III, and the neoclassical architecture so loved by postmodernists—all these elements have been churning around in her imagination for sixty years. She fused them together in an enchanting way, inspiring numerous followers. But her brilliant originality, while making her work instantly and unmistakably recognizable, has also made it impossible to be copied. Madeleine Castaing is inimitable. She is also smart, interesting, and unforgettably eccentric. To meet her, in her heavenly albeit crumbling surroundings, dressed in some odd costume and wearing her famous wig, held on by a chin strap, and enormous false eyelashes, confirms all one's hopes. She is personally as original as her decorating style, a style that combines antiquity and freshness in a mysterious way.

Renzo Mongiardino

"I AM NOT A DECORATOR. I'M A CREATOR OF ambience, a scenic designer, an architect, but *not* a decorator." That's what Renzo Mongiardino said to John Richardson, who in turn calls him the master illusionist. David Hicks has said that Mongiardino is the greatest living decorator. To most people, stupefied as they behold the rooms that he mysteriously conjures up from heaven knows what fantastic sources, using methods known only to him, Mongiardino must seem more like an alchemist than anything else. Otherwise, how could he manufacture ancient, disintegrating materials that stand up to the upholsterer's handling? Or the frescoed walls, inlaid panels, and carved friezes (if indeed they *are* carved!) that transform twentieth-century rooms into dense, silent reveries of the past? If you feel, upon entering one of his fantastic rooms, like a spectator accidentally pushed onto a stage

The colors of this stupendous drawing room in Paris might have been inspired by a Titian. It is difficult to say how such grandeur can be so cozy, but that is part of Mongiardino's genius.

set prepared for a moment of Puccini or Verdi, you wouldn't be totally off course. In his career, he has indeed designed the staging of *Tosca*, *The Taming of the Shrew*, and *Don Pasquale*, as well as doing film work with Franco Zeffirelli. But his training is in architecture. And if you saw him, you would think he belonged to the faculty of a university in some remote place. This impression would not be dispelled by his manner of speaking. It would be impossible to place him in the hectic world of many of his Croesus-like clients whose preoccupation with money and rank must surely perplex him. Ironically, Mongiardino is himself a symbol of money and rank, and the list of those able to hire him reads like the names of donors carved into the walls at the entrance of a great museum. Even if Mrs. John Heinz II, for whom Mongiardino has done enchanting work, swears that he isn't nearly as expensive as Jansen was, to most eyes, his work appears to float in that stratospheric region where cost no longer matters. All those Thyssens, Agnellis, and Rothschilds, however, don't seem to faze him. He lives and works in Milan in a world that is made up of equal parts of his inherited past and his brilliantly created present.

Renzo Mongiardino was born in 1916 in Genoa, where his parents lived in a beautiful palazzo. If you haven't seen Genoa, you cannot imagine the rich combination of the medieval town, the enormous, historic port, the spectacular Renaissance and baroque Via Garibaldi, and finally, throughout the town, the monumental evidence of its vast nineteenth-century prosperity. Grand houses, unchanged for three hundred years, with frescoed wall decorations and illusionistic ceilings of tremendous charm, still exist, owned by descendants of their builders. This great,

Lee Radziwill's country bedroom in Buckinghamshire was decorated in Mongiardino's version of the farmhouse style. Gingham and quilts and painted floors are predictably different under his direction than they would be anywhere else.

cosmopolitan port city, quite far from Rome, is the place where Mongiardino's deep vision began to take form.

When it came time to go to university, he went to Milan to study architecture and has stayed there ever since. A profound feeling of harmony with the past and a tenacious ability to work through the problems of production equipped him for the direction he took toward scenic design and interior decoration. His temperament makes it more enjoyable for him to spend time with artisans than with other people, and his dedicated band of craftsmen are somehow able to disperse themselves all over Europe and the United States so that he can decorate houses in New York, Paris, London, and in all corners of Italy. Jansen operated out of a seven-story headquarters in Paris. Mongiardino, by way of comparison, works out of his flat in Milan. Of course he *does* have assistants in Paris and New York. But the mystery of how he works is as riveting as the work itself.

The first memory I have of Mongiardino's work is still very clear. I saw a photograph of a library in the farmhouse owned by Count and Countess Brando Brandolini, not far from Venice. It is a very pure room decorated in the style of Charles X, with *bois clair* Gothic Revival woodwork, furniture of the same pale wood, and a great deal of dark green velvet. When I visited it in person twenty-five years later, the room was unchanged and even more beautiful than in its photographs. It made me wonder if Mongiardino was at all inspired by the work of Madeleine Castaing, who has often worked in the Charles X style. The wall panels, edged in elaborate borders, and the close stylistic relationship of all the furniture remind one of the work of Madame Castaing, as does the carpet woven in floral squares in imitation of needlepoint. In his later work Mongiardino has shown a much less dogmatic attitude toward the single period of a room. His interiors have become far more loosely organized in terms of their stylistic range. In that respect, they are more inventive and more romantic, and they elicit in the viewer an intense feeling of curiosity. Are those walls stamped Córdoba leather? No, they just look as though they are.

In the early sixties Lee Radziwill, whose grasp of decorating is innate and marvelously broad-ranged, became intrigued by photographs of Mongiardino's rooms. From London, where the Radziwills lived in a small Georgian brick house in the neighborhood of Buckingham Palace, Lee wrote to Mongiardino in Milan, asking if he would be interested in coming to London to help her with a very long, narrow, difficult drawing room. Included in the letter was a description of the room. In the ensuing correspondence, arrangements were made for Mongiardino to travel to London to discuss the project. When he arrived, he had with him three complete schemes, any one of which, according to Lee, would have been perfect. The one chosen was a proposal for an "orientalist" fantasy in which the walls were intricately paneled and bordered with block-printed Indian paisley cotton. Against the highly complicated background of pattern and color were melon-colored taffeta undercurtains, velvet sofas, a plain brown (and very English) carpet, and a lot of good eighteenth-century French furniture, some of it in gilt. The casual mixture of inexpensive materials, elaborately applied and used with exquisite furniture and pictures, gave the room a playful richness that struck precisely the right note. Many of the rooms one sees decorated in this fashion take on the atmosphere of a high-camp opium den. The Radziwills' drawing room was precious and refined but nonetheless amusing. In their dining room, Mongiardino used panels of counterfeit Córdoba leather bought right off the set of an opera production.

From this auspicious beginning, there followed a house in Oxfordshire and a Fifth Avenue apartment, all decorated by Mongiardino for the Radziwills. The house in the country is a simple architectural affair, part of which had been a bake house in the eighteenth century. Fearing that it was too simple for Mongiardino, the Radziwills asked if he felt he could ever find

The Charles X library of the Brandolinis outside Venice is a perfect example of Mongiardino's fusion of architecture and decoration. Its appeal is as great now as it was thirty years ago.

it interesting enough to work on. Far from rejecting the offer, he set out to create a delicately complex interpretation of a farmhouse somewhere (but clearly not Oxfordshire!) in the middle of the nineteenth century. Flowers were everywhere, real and invented. The tour de force, however, was the dining room, inspired by an illustration in Mario Praz's *An Illustrated History of Furnishing*, published in 1964, which has been a bible to many decorators, as it certainly has been for Mongiardino. Sicilian scarves printed with flowers on a background of intense blue were pasted onto the walls. Over the scarves, Mongiardino's lifelong friend and collaborator, Lila de Nobili, painted more flowers and portraits of the Radziwill children.

The master bedroom was an essay in gingham checks and patchwork quilts, two materials that Mongiardino loves and uses over and over. But don't think of an Amish farmhouse! The effect, as usual, was one of skillful needlework, a lot of special effects, and a fearless determination to achieve an arresting level of elaborate decoration. The painted floor, another Mongiardino staple, managed to blend his love of handcraft with his passion for pattern.

There is no limit to this passion. Two other Indian print rooms I remember—one for the Brandolinis in Venice, the other for Count and Countess Rudolfo Crespi in Rome—clearly illustrated Mongiardino's capacity to rework a theme in another setting with very different results. In New York, the stenciled paintwork that he commissioned for the staircase of Mrs. John Heinz's townhouse proves that pattern can be far more useful as a background than solid color. At Daylesford, the Oxfordshire house built for Warren Hastings, decorated by John Fowler for the Rothermeres, and then bought by Baron Thyssen, Mongiardino stenciled one room to resemble ivory or marble fretwork, a fabulous allusion (and illusion) to Hastings's career in India. In another room at Daylesford there was a huge, tufted banquette covered in damask, the color and texture of which had been altered by many hours spent applying a bright blue Pentel pen. (Actually, it must have taken dozens of Pentels.) The effect was very funny and yet very beautiful.

At the same time, not all Mongiardino rooms are pattern-filled. In the principal dining room in the Crespis' Rome flat, a series of rooms in a palazzo with all the right palatial proportions, he did the walls, curtains, and furniture all in dark green velvet, in the midst of which stood great gilded console tables.

Mongiardino's way with velvet is endlessly inventive and can be strangely rich. The drawing-room walls of the Radziwills' New York apartment were upholstered in raspberry-colored velvet, with an added band of scrollwork up and down the corners and around the top and bottom of the room. This border had been painted directly on the velvet and, over the years, it became more and more muted, achieving a look of age far greater, of course, than its actual years. This splendid apartment on two floors was, I suppose, the first work Mongiardino did in New York. There would be a lot more.

Since the early sixties, when the Radziwill flat was remodeled and redecorated, Mongiardino has worked on the beautiful Heinz house designed by Mott Schmidt. In it, he has combined bits of decoration from a previous Jansen job done for the Heinzes with new elements of his own invention. Added to all of this is a superb collection of nineteenth-century French pictures.

He has also decorated New York apartments for Gianni and Marella Agnelli, Stavros Niarchos, and, recently, for Peter Sharp. Anyone familiar with the building Mr. Sharp lives in is immediately aware of the changes brought about by Mongiardino's hand. All the doors have been shifted around, including the front door. The hall has been foreshortened by columns, which makes it seem a taller, better setting for the huge Guido Reni picture that used to hang in Spencer House in London.

Everywhere you look, in every room you enter, there are Mongiardino finishes on walls and furniture that defy accurate comprehension: painted and polished plaster that looks like scagliola; trompe l'oeil marble, parquet, and inlaid paneling; bookcases with marble plaques of many colors and damask cut up and sewn back together with inserted borders, ending up with the look of something from the 1660s at Ham House. Most recently, Mongiardino has installed for Peter a room executed in paint but done to resemble the pictorial intarsia of the fifteenth and sixteenth centuries in Italy, most notably the one by Baccio Pontelli in the ducal palace at Urbino. But this room is not based on a single design program. It contains references to modern New York, Renaissance Italy, and objects from Peter Sharp's own collection, placed on the illusionistic shelf that girdles the room. Over the library table in the center hangs a Mongiardino-made gaming-table lamp, modified for its non-game-table use and very close in design to an old one in Madeleine Castaing's Paris flat. I mention Madame Castaing again because no one else (except for the pages of Mario Praz) could be said to have influenced Mongiardino. The carpet in Giancarlo Giammetti's bedroom suite in his stupendous Tuscan house, decorated a few years ago by Mongiardino, is of the same design as one of Madame Castaing's in Paris, based on trellis fretwork.

The most elaborate and sumptuous work of Mongiardino's I have seen is the series of rooms he decorated in the Hôtel Lambert, the seventeenth-century Parisian *hôtel* that belongs to Baron and Baronne Guy de Rothschild. Even the rooms of Daylesford, filled as they were with fabulous Thyssen pictures hanging on walls that had been stenciled, glazed, and appliquéed in an innumerable variety of techniques—even those rooms seemed relaxed and normal compared to the staggering luxury of the Rothschilds' apartment. To see it after trying to absorb the forty-year-old decorations upstairs executed by Emilio Terry and Georges Geoffroy for Baron de Redé can cause a frantic breakdown of one's ability to remember what one looked at merely thirty seconds before. If the ancient purpose of palace decoration was to subdue subjects and rivals alike, how that practice worked becomes very clear.

The atmosphere, however, is one of pleasure, not of oppressive grandeur. All the Sèvres and Majolica, Augsburg gold, and old master paintings in the splendid historic architecture of Le Vau is neither overshadowed nor underplayed by Mongiardino's decoration. He possesses a rare sympathy for palace decoration, nowhere more splendidly revealed than in the Rothschild rooms of the Hôtel Lambert.

At home in Milan, he lives and works in an apartment completely of his own design that resembles the habitation of some cozy bishop or cardinal. An opera-loving one at that. As usual, there is very little hint of the outdoors. To a great degree, they are rooms for introspection, rooms for study. They exist for and were created by a man who accords his work the highest respect and reverence. How else could he *do* it?

David Hicks

I N 1961, WHEN I FIRST WORKED FOR DAVID
Hicks, his style was in the process of coming into
the sharp focus that would make it recognizable to
anyone interested in decorating for the next fifteen
years. It was a style, as the New York decorator (whose work
I admire) Bob Bray said recently, that influenced *everybody*. Here
in the United States, in England, in France, and even in Spain,
David Hicks imitators existed in droves. His name itself became
a generic label for a huge category of geometric designs.

The London shop he occupied thirty years ago, in Lowndes
Street just off Cadogan Square, had two large windows in which
he displayed bold assemblages lit with terrific drama. These still
lifes might include architectural elements, hunks of garden or-
nament, or decorative objects from all parts of the world, their
sole link being that David Hicks liked them. His exceptional

*The present-day country
drawing room of Lady Pam-
ela and David Hicks is a
softer version of the decorative style that he pioneered in
the sixties. The sharp contrast between richness and
simplicity gives this room its
great energy.*

skill at combining otherwise unrelated artifacts endowed these arrangements with an exciting freshness that caught many eyes. More than anyone else at the time, he used theatrical lighting to further his dramatic creations. His love of conspicuous drama was always central to his style. Even his car in those days, a big, tan, American Ford convertible, stood out in the London world of Minis. Like practically everything else to do with the Hicks style of the sixties, that car was a statement against the old-fashioned canons of staid English taste. Of course, 1961 was the beginning of a vast movement in England that spread a youthful message of revolt all over the world. From the Beatles to Mary Quant to David Bailey, the variety of new English style that flowed out of London to the rest of the world was exciting and tremendously powerful. At thirty-two, David Hicks was still young enough to fit into the category of precocious tastemakers who were destined to drive people middle-aged or older almost crazy with the desire to appear younger than they really were. The era of old knees showing under the hems of miniskirts had begun.

To anyone who knows David Hicks, his personality is marked by a love of facts and details and a minute knowledge of the things he cares about. If it is a great house, he must know who designed it, who built it, and when. If it is a portrait, he has to find out the name of the painter, the sitter, whom it belonged to, and all the places it has hung. The mystery of the porphyry tetrarchs huddling in the corner of St. Mark's in Venice has always fascinated him. Yet he hated school and now says that he never really learned anything while he was there. From Chartwell, where he spent his teenage years, he went to the Central School of Arts and Crafts in London, where he continued to daydream about becoming the greatest contemporary English artist. His father, who was in his sixties when David was born, had died in 1941 and Mrs. Hicks (who had the lovely name of Iris), certain that her son would find a career sooner in London than in Essex, where he had grown up, eventually sold her house in Coggeshall and bought one in South Eaton Place. That was 1953, and David by then had finished art school, been in the Army, and was temporarily employed by the advertising firm of J. Walter Thompson. He had hated the army, and he hated J. Walter Thompson, but he loved houses, and when his mother turned their new London house over to him to decorate, events began to move swiftly and significantly. Overnight, as he says in his book *Living With Design*, he became a decorator.

By the time he was eleven or twelve, David Hicks was absorbed by the houses he saw. One in particular impressed upon him the marvelous possibilities of interior decoration. It was a big Victorian house belonging to friends of his parents and it had been taken in hand by Lady Eaton and Geoffrey Holme. What they did to the house in the way of color (vivid and bright) and arrangement (complex and highly organized) astonished the young eyes of the Hickses' little boy. Sporting equipment hung on the hall walls like baroque trophies, and dozens of silhouettes massed together in one room obviously touched a nerve in the brain of this child whose own gift for arranging things would be renowned in twenty years. There were many more influences to come.

To name them chronologically would be a bore. But the early influences went more or less like this: Syrie Maugham, Rory Cameron, Van Truex, Emilio Terry, Charles de Beistegui, Madeleine Castaing, and Billy Baldwin. And one must certainly mention Mrs. Joshua Cosden and the Countess of Portarlington. Finally, David mentions often the tremendous contribution (both general and specific) of John Fowler. Again and again, when the subject of color is discussed, he places Fowler at the head of the list of great colorists of this century. (The contemporary figure in decorating whose sense of color he most admires is the Englishman Alec Cobbe, by the way.) Thirty years or more ago, however, it might seem that the Hicks style was running more or less counter to that of John Fowler. David was, in his own words, dedicated to "clean lines and pure design." If not quite a modernist manifesto, that statement at least points to a distaste for old chintz and pleasing decay.

The house in South Eaton Place did not evoke many of the influences that would come into play a few years later when the Hicks look finally reached its easily recognizable state. But this 1953 expression of his taste was still a precursor of his coming style. Its principal impact lay in the shocking colors that were juxtaposed in combinations that further intensified their impact: for example, a scarlet sofa with grass-green fringe and pillows in two shades of yellow. Over the sofa were a dozen or more pictures of various shapes and types with frames and mats of an equally varied and colorful nature. The walls and carpet were grey. This arrangement of pictures on a dark wall called to mind, more than anyone else, William Pahlmann. In another room in the same house, a fabulous Gothic Revival chair, designed by William Porden for Eaton Hall, covered in lilac and placed against red walls and Bristol-blue curtains, conveyed a more prophetic message of the Hicks future. Nineteenth-century architectural drawings and landscapes in old frames were hung in a far more structured manner. In the back of the Gothic chair,

Twenty-five years ago, the London drawing room of the Londonderrys captured the attention of an entire generation of imitators of the Hicks style.

a Victorian flowered needlework pillow in shades of red, pink, and aubergine was a harbinger, almost forty years ago, of a mixture of tones which has been the basis of color schemes for David Hicks ever since.

Fortunately for David, one of the first people to see the house was Peter Coats, who was then an editor of *House & Garden*. Within a few months, these startling rooms appeared in the pages of *House & Garden* and the telephone in South Eaton Place began to ring. David Hicks was in business.

His first client was the former wife of the late Condé Nast, an American woman from Chicago. His first partner was Tom Parr, the current proprietor of Colefax & Fowler. The remaining years of the fifties were filled with travels in the course of which David met the people and saw the monuments that would influence him from then on. Rory Cameron and the house he remodeled in Saint-Jean-Cap-Ferrat for his mother in the late forties had a profound effect on the Hicks philosophy. La Fiorentina, as this most fabled of houses is called, was considered by everyone who saw it to be just about the chicest house in the world. While Lady Kenmare (the owner) was upstairs trying to decide which diamond pin to wear to dinner (that's David's explanation of why she was always late; Dominick Dunne has another theory), her son Rory was busy entertaining their friends in rooms of heroic scale and precise simplicity. His taste in architecture, objects, and gardens was for strong design with a deceptively plain appearance that belied a love of rich luxury. Modern French carpets from Cogolin, solid-colored materials, severe curtains, a preference for cotton and linen rather than for silk—these characteristics of Rory's taste were entirely sympathetic to David's increasingly clear view.

Toward the end of the fifties, two important changes took place. First, David became engaged to the Lady Pamela Mountbatten, first cousin of Prince Philip, more distant cousin of the Queen, and daughter of Lord and Lady Mountbatten. At more or less the same time, Tom Parr left to join Colefax & Fowler. So David Hicks, suddenly on his own and engaged to a royally connected heiress, moved into another realm of fame and importance. The wedding took place in January 1960 and the wedding party was photographed by *Life* magazine.

The scarlet sofa with the green fringe was recovered in a

small-patterned, dark brown material trimmed with a fringe of another shade of brown and moved into the study of the new Hicks flat. The architectural drawings were hung on brown velvet walls along with stone fragments of classical carvings. In all this deep, shadowy monochrome, gilt frames and bronze and ormolu objects reflected the focused pools of light that were one of the trademarks of David Hicks rooms. The drawing room, in strong contrast to the study, had white walls and a dark aubergine carpet. Shocking pink, acid green, and yellow were concentrated on chair covers and flowers.

English decorators and their imitators have usually preferred natural, blowsy-looking bouquets. Monsieur Boudin, on the other hand, arranged flowers in color groupings that contained elements of the scheme of both the room in which the flowers were placed and the room seen beyond. David, however, bunched flowers together in graphic masses that more and more often matched the color of the surrounding objects on the table top. Gathering together all sorts of things of a related color had been a favorite ploy of Rory Cameron as well as the tremendously stylish Winnie Portarlington, an Australian heiress who married the Earl of Portarlington, was a great friend of Edward VIII and Mrs. Simpson, and finally lived, in London and in Ascot, in houses of fabulous twentieth-century chic. Echoes of the twenties and thirties filled all of her rooms. In her country drawing room, with its brown satin sofas and Marion Dorn carpet, jade pieces were arranged according to color on brown lacquer trays. Her dining-room chair seats were of needlepoint worked in simple geometric patterns of brown and string color. On the drawing board of David Hicks's office in 1961, more intricate geometric designs were being developed for the new carpets that

would play a major role in spreading the fame of the Hicks style.

The first prototype of these designs to come off the looms was one of interlocking Y's woven in tobacco brown, black, and cream. The testing ground for this pattern was the back stairway of a great Georgian house of the 1720s that was being restored by the Hickses and that would become within the year a finished ideal of a personal taste, the embodiment of a contemporary synthesis of old and new design. Grand one moment and understated the next, Britwell Salome, as this lovely house is called, was while David and Pamela lived there "the epitome of a 1960s response to the past, a response that is in large part of David Hicks's own creation." This is taken from a 1972 article in *Country*

Life written by Gervase Jackson-Stops. Certainly it was a superb house in every way.

Britwell Salome, which is not far from Oxford, is a big house that gives the appearance of being rather small. Because it was built by a Roman Catholic bachelor (in the 1720s), it has very few bedrooms and a ravishing private chapel that was added somewhat later and was used as the dining room by the Hickses. Legend has it that the architect worked under Hawksmoor, and numerous strong details of the interior point to this tantalizing possibility. It is all the more appropriate since David is a keen devotee of the work of Nicholas Hawksmoor and even designed a library twenty-five years ago for an unfinished room at Hawksmoor's Easton Neston, the breathtaking house of Lord Hesketh, whose mother is an old friend of David's.

The interior of Britwell, because of the plan of the house, allowed David to create rooms of a self-contained nature. With the exception of the view from the front door across the baroque Doric hall and on out the central drawing-room window beyond, there are no continuous vistas that require a specific, flowing relationship from one scheme to the next. So the seven principal rooms on the main floor had distinctly individual moods. The hall colors were dark brown, white, and stone, emphasizing its masculine, architectural quality. Directly ahead was the drawing room, with its free mixture of Louis XVI chairs and settee, William Kent table, and the low-backed Tuxedo sofas (as we call them) that David has used so often. The colors ranged from the cream background tone to greens, pinks, and reds, at first, and then later more neutral shades as upholstery materials were changed. Abstract paintings and an absence of mirrors on the walls, which were upholstered in the same cream material as the curtains, reinforced the modern *idea* of the room, yet the richness of the traditional elements prevented it from being dogmatically contemporary. It was a room that, like the rooms of Syrie Maugham thirty-five years earlier, had a great effect on American decorators. Billy Baldwin, Albert Hadley, and even Mrs. Parish showed signs in their work of a very clear awareness of what was going on in the Hicks office. Mrs Parish's new Fifth Avenue drawing room back in the seventies, with aubergine walls, lots of white upholstery, lavender curtains edged in geranium red, and modern paintings in clear, compatible colors, might not have lasted for very long, but while it existed, it was beautiful proof of the irresistible style of the time. Similarly, Natalie Davenport, the most style-conscious of the McMillen ladies, decorated a handsome Sutton Place apartment for her daughter in a mood based on many Hicks themes. Nowadays, the work of John Stefanidis continues the tradition of Hicks influence.

But back to Britwell. The hall and the drawing room occupy the middle of the central block. In the four corners are a splendid stair hall, a small octagonal room, a library, and another small sitting room. The stair hall, a tour de force of exquisitely carved woodwork, was papered in the famous blue and white vase pattern taken by David from a fragment of seventeenth-century Portuguese damask. The octagonal room had, as its reason for existing, a delicious Batty Langley Gothic chimney and a big drinks table. There was also a center table. It was not a place to sit. The library, in the opposite corner, with one window and lots of wall space completely covered with bookcases filled with books (which, over time, were increasingly dominated by red bindings as David rebound more and more of the volumes in every possible shade of crimson, scarlet, and vermilion), was otherwise decorated in black and grey. Finally, the so-called Rex Whistler room occupied the front corner opposite the stair hall. Its walls had been furred out and its ceiling lowered to accommodate a cycle of painted panels by Rex Whistler from the Mountbattens' 1937 Brook House flat in London. All in pale blue-green, silver, and grisaille, these heavenly panels (which are now in the dining room of the Hickses' third home, a Regency house nearby) depict family seats of the Battenbergs and the Cassels, Lady Pamela's paternal and maternal families. The delicate color scheme and fragile quality of the white taffeta curtains and the white quilted Syrie Maugham sofa, in addition to the refinement of the celadon and blanc de chine objects, carried the actual functional mood (that of a lady's private retreat) to an exquisite level that reminded one of a room that might have been occupied by the Marquise de Pompadour in a modern incarnation.

Along the walls of the cream-paneled upstairs hall stood a large set of red japanned Giles Grendy chairs, also from Brook House. That grand penthouse had been decorated in the thirties by Nell Cosden, an American woman best remembered for the Palm Beach house she decorated for her very rich husband and herself. Her brilliant ability to put furniture of marvelous quality in sleek thirties rooms was an inspiration to David when he saw on the one hand photographs of her work and, on the other, the actual pieces of English furniture—the chairs and mirrors and console tables—that in the sixties were in the Mountbatten house in Wilton Crescent. Mrs. Cosden and David finally met at the end of her life, when she lived at the Dakota in New York. Her charm and style remained for him undimmed, and her food was superb. Like Billy Baldwin, David has always taken

This William Kent period table, now in the drawing room of Mr. and Mrs. Oscar de la Renta, was loaded with red objects—porphyry, leather, and stone—and placed under a red contemporary painting twenty years ago.

the food of a great house into account when discussing taste and style. Flowers, food, fragrances—these aspects of housekeeping, ephemeral though they may seem, are vital parts of the whole, chic household. Automobiles and clothes had better be carefully considered, too. And then there's the question of livery. And more and more in his career, David Hicks has concerned himself with the subject of gardens.

Ten minutes away from Britwell, along the narrow roads

of the Oxfordshire countryside, lived Nancy Lancaster in her enchanting house, Haseley, with its very beautiful garden. Another half an hour or so away was John Fowler, hidden away down a bumpy country lane, surrounded by *his* divine garden. And over the years the garden at Britwell grew in scope and formality, taking on French qualities here and English ones there. Like Rory Cameron, who could create a garden inspired by Williamsburg on a terrace overlooking the Mediterranean, David took inspiration from all over the place. One might find him dogmatic in his speech, but never in his unpredictable, unfettered view of the world around him.

Throughout the sixties and into the seventies he worked constantly on houses and flats that left a steady wave of influence in their wake. Alexander Albrizzi and Tony Cloughley furthered the style. A little later, the work of François Catroux (along with that of a lot of other Frenchmen) began to reflect the design message of David Hicks. Angelo Donghia's style was greatly affected by it, and in San Francisco, John Dickenson, in a way always original and personal, adopted many Hicks traits. I might add that David Hicks was in turn influenced by John Dickenson, so the flow of ideas went back and forth.

The list of David's clients during these years covered names from a wide variety of worlds. Londonderry, Cholmondely, Dashwood, Brabourne (in-laws), and Channon were all part of the category of people whose houses usually possessed built-in architectural and decorative distinction. The Londonderrys' drawing room in town was published over and over again. Its white curtains with red bows in the shape of Maltese crosses were copied by eager decorators everywhere. The floor was covered with a larger-scale than usual Hicks geometric carpet that became one of his staple patterns.

Then there were clients from all kinds of businesses, the director Stanley Donen and his beautiful American wife, the restaurateur and collector Keith Leichtenstein, and Peter Saunders. I mention these people because their houses had remarkable impact and were published in French, English, and American magazines. The magazine *L'Oeil* in Paris, for a time the superb brain (and eye) child of Rosamond Bernier, played a unique part in spreading the fame of David Hicks. In photographs, both black and white and color, and all of a uniformly high standard of beauty, *L'Oeil* documented the development of his work more sympathetically than any other publication. Madame Bernier was a link in the Rory Cameron–Billy Baldwin chain of friendships, and at this stage of David's work he and Pamela bought a house in a town in the south of France, not too far a drive from the orbit of La Fiorentina. Its pale, bleached-out interiors called to mind rooms by Syrie Maugham and Rory Cameron and even Winnie Portarlington's rented summer house in the thirties which she hired Fortnum and Mason to decorate entirely in white. Like Britwell, the house in Roquebrune appeared in a dozen different magazines. The bathtub in one of the bedroom suites was particularly appealing, placed, like Jefferson's bed at Monticello, in a niche opening onto two different rooms, one for bathing, the other for dressing. The materials used for curtains and upholstery were cotton or linen. The carpets were Cogolin straw and white textured wool.

David Hicks took the English decorating tradition of liking modest materials even further, almost eliminating rich materials altogether in many of his designs, or turning the concept of luxurious materials on its head by using silk velvet on the walls of a room in which all the furniture was covered in printed cotton. He once said not to worry about where to use moiré—"Just *never* use it!" Dyeing obviously new silk in order to make it look old was often done as well.

Now, almost forty years after his career began, the David Hicks firm operates in a number of different countries out of offices more or less under his guidance. At home, his attention is focused on building and garden design projects. A huge Palladian house in Portugal with porticoes on four sides inspired by the Inigo Jones church in Covent Garden was completed a few years ago. Its garden grows each year with the addition of terraces and fountains. More recently, he has finished a Gothic folly for himself, a tower with a workroom on the lower floor and a library above, each wall of which has a different ogee-shaped window so that, seen from outside, no two elevations are the same. At the end of the ever lengthening vista stretching off into the distance from the Hickses' dining-room windows (the room where the Rex Whistler panels now hang), there are two new Coade stone sphinxes, which inspired the cook to comment, "Those sheep haven't moved for two days. Are they sick?" Someday there will probably be a column or a pyramid in the distance. Thoughts of Charles de Beistegui or William Beckford are never out of David Hicks's head for long. Meanwhile, he plants another hundred roses here, another thousand trees there, and when he comes in at night he rearranges the objects on the top of a superb table or a commode as only he can do it, making certain that whoever is about to arrive—whether a guest or one of the Hickses' three grown and very amusing children—will find something new and alive in the room. His interest never flags.

Michael Taylor

URING THE THIRTY YEARS OF HIS CAREER, Michael Taylor investigated a rich variety of design approaches, ending finally with a look that was recognizable to everyone as "the Michael Taylor style." He was (and is) widely imitated, especially on the West Coast. The type of interior decoration that he developed into almost a formula is very American—in fact, very Californian, with its sunny, open-air informality and its thirties, movie-star glamour. C. Ray Smith, in his book *Interior Design in the Twentieth Century*, written with Allen Tate, called Taylor a thirties revivalist, and the all-white Michael Taylor room was indeed a trademark twenty years ago. At the end of his life, however, those whose knowledge of Michael Taylor's decorating was limited to his late work would have thought of him as a designer of rooms characterized by rusticity, overscale, and a beachy kind

The San Francisco house of Mr. and Mrs. Gorham Knowles was one of Michael Taylor's last jobs. The garden room, with its gigantic terms representing the four seasons, stone walls, stone tables, and marble floors, shows his love of strong masonry used indoors.

of luxury only to be found along the Pacific coast. But two of his last jobs harked back to his earliest themes. One is an evocation of Elsie Mendl in her Beverly Hills days, even including some of the nightclubby furniture from her Villa Trianon party room that the New York antiques dealer Anthony Victoria had acquired in 1981. The other (both houses are in San Francisco) is an Art Deco house decorated in a way that, on the one hand, is sympathetic to the almost Busby Berkeley architecture of the house and, on the other, provides a perfect background for the brand-new, up-to-the-minute contemporary art collected by the owners. All of this work illustrates a dictum of Taylor's expressed in his essay in the 1964 book *The Finest Rooms*: "It is contrast that brings things excitingly alive." The central contrast of his work is that of his originality combined with the influences that inspired him.

In the thirties and forties, when Michael Taylor was growing up in the country town of Santa Rosa, north of San Francisco, three of the great decorators of the century were working in northern California. All that was going on in this rarified atmosphere seems to have soaked right into the brain of Michael Taylor. Syrie Maugham decorated the fabulous David Adler house of Mrs. Tobin Clark in San Mateo in the early thirties. Frances Elkins, Adler's sister and colleague on many jobs, was in full swing, working from her legendary studio in Monterey. And, in a building on Russian Hill in San Francisco, Jean-Michel Frank, whose creations trickled into the work of both Mrs. Maugham and Mrs. Elkins, had designed a dazzling apartment for Mr. Templeton Crocker. The impact of these three famous talents on Michael Taylor was immeasurable. Throughout his career he constantly referred to their innovations in varying degrees. A fourth influence must have been the lobby of the

Fairmont Hotel, decorated in a somewhat bizarre interpretation of Venetian baroque crossed with the Second Empire—all the brainchild of Dorothy Draper in the forties.

Taylor's parents, as the story goes, wanted him to be a doctor, a typical example of the crazy extremes of thinking that plague people whose sons want to be decorators. Michael knew better. He worked for a furniture dealer, took courses in decorating at the Rudolf Schaeffer School and, in 1951, at the age of twenty-five, went into business with Francis Mihailoff. That partnership lasted four years.

In 1956 he set out on his own. For four years he worked away on a number of houses and apartments that, individually, illustrated the major themes of his style. This style, with its profound indebtedness to the sophisticated chic of the previous two decades, encompassed a wide variety of design elements, all of which were combined in a bold, extravagant manner. For example, in one house Taylor decorated, he mixed Victorian and French provincial furniture against backgrounds dominated by white—white paint, white rugs, and fresh white finishes on the armoires and chair frames. Like Frances Elkins, who had died in 1953 and many of whose models Michael Taylor had bought, he upholstered white painted chairs in white quilted linen with elaborate blue trim repeating the color of the blue and white porcelain used as the only color accent in the room. Both Frances Elkins and Michael Taylor preferred two-color rooms; one of those colors was light and neutral, often white. And they both favored the use of one pattern in a scheme rather than the casual-looking mixture of several different patterns. This formula, if one may call it that, was also a favorite of Billy Baldwin's. Mrs. Elkins was the inspiration for both Billy and Michael, as were the soft, plump upholstery designs of Syrie Maugham. Where Michael Taylor's rooms differed from Billy's, however, was in their generally overscaled aspect. Billy was tiny; Michael was big. Billy's rooms usually had a spare, cool quality. Michael's were voluptuous and paradoxically warm, given their cool, pale schemes. Not that he avoided dark rooms altogether. In some cases, he would fill rooms with highly saturated dark colors and rough-hewn wood—big beams, rustic furniture, and crude trellises or shutters. In photographs of one or two houses of this sort there is a primitive, almost Gothic quality that makes one think of Bernard Maybeck, the California arts and crafts architect, who died in 1957.

Another Michael Taylor exercise in glamour and nostalgia that appeared in photographs published over and over again was a bedroom setting created as a conscious homage to Syrie Maugham, who had died in 1955. Using a chinoiserie canopy bed with bamboo turned posts that had once belonged to Mrs. Maugham, he piled her trademarks one on top of another—a Venetian mirror, tufted chairs, white materials, bows, shells, and painted plaster forms for lamps and andirons—in a condensed fashion that summed up his whole knockout attitude toward overstatement. It was hard not to get the point.

One person who got the point and has kept it all along is Mrs. Thomas Kempner. She and her husband bought their New York apartment in the late 1950s, shortly after Taylor had set out on his own. Mrs. Kempner's mother, a Frances Elkins devotee and client, had become an early mentor to Michael Taylor. As a result of their long friendship, Nan Kempner and Michael Taylor went to work together on the plans for the new apartment. To a large degree, the results of their collaboration are

This dark, rustic house was made even more dramatic by black, anthracite, and zebra-skin upholstery. It is entirely a California style.

still intact; over the years, it became a bellwether of the developing Taylor style. There is a guest room with enchanting copies of the Syrie Maugham chinoiserie bed and walls hung with Chinese wallpaper. Taylor loved Chinese paper and painted silk wall hangings and used them in three of the Kempner rooms. Two of his last dining rooms were papered with exquisite antique Chinese panels.

The Kempner drawing room is dominated by huge tufted banquettes and a Syrie Maugham tufted sofa, all covered in honey-colored ribbed velvet, a longtime Taylor favorite material. One wall is covered by a big Coromandel screen. The carpet was originally a colorless, faded Aubusson (now disintegrated and replaced). Instead of curtains at the windows on two walls of this corner room, there are paneled shutters like those one would find in an eighteenth-century house. Their severity establishes that contraposition in this otherwise sensual room that Taylor so loved. Rope-twist chairs finished in gold leaf and marvelous gilt wall lights, all from Frederick Victoria, who was one of Taylor's favorite furniture dealers, add brightness and richness, as well as more contrast, to the all-over fawn color of the walls and upholstery and the black ground of the screen and the velvet on the gold chairs. Suede and fur pillows introduce a sort of Sunset Boulevard note into the atmosphere of this moody room.

Upstairs, the master bedroom has more superb Chinese wallpaper, a pair of Italian rococo commodes, and a set of Louis XVI painted chairs, all of which are mixed together in the manner favored by both Michael Taylor and Mrs. Kempner. His last room in this apartment is an upstairs sitting room decorated in his late style, with giant Italian wicker furniture and Japanese screens.

In what could be called a posthumous collaboration with some of the great decorators of the past, Michael Taylor established his original style. It was not the style of blue-haired old ladies. Although full of opulent European furniture from the eighteenth century, this style was essentially American, even Californian, in its lavish but informal point of view. Everything that appeared on the decorating scene was a candidate for Taylor assimilation. His famous sofa with its enormous rolled arms, for instance, was based on the design of one he bought directly from Denning & Fourcade. In his last years, he drew his inspiration from the designs of young craftsmen, one of whom, Mimi London, supplied him with ideas and prototypes of furniture and accessories that shaped his most widely imitated style—his rustic Pacific look. The seeds of this brand of decorating had existed, of course, from early on in his career. Big plants, Mexican craft chairs covered in pigskin, trellises, shutters, beams—all these rough elements appeared over the years in his beach-house designs and in a fabulous restaurant that was also tented in a coarsely printed copy of the Madeleine Castaing Grand Arbre pattern that Billy Baldwin used in Diana Vreeland's living room (in red) and bedroom (in blue). When Michael met Mimi London in the early seventies, things really took off. First, she started selling minerals, especially big geodes. Michael loved them and wanted to have the best ones. Then she made a table out of a cypress tree trunk. He had to have some of those too. (Over the years, Mimi sold 8,000 tree-trunk tables.) On a trip to Montana, she made a log chair for herself which Michael adored and added to his list of staples in a number of designs. When he wanted a poster bed made of logs, she assembled one on a flatbed truck. These huge, virile pieces of furniture were used with equally huge pieces of Italian wicker furniture, tables made of stone sitting on stone floors, and numerous oriental artifacts. Michael's fondness for Asian decorative objects, a San Francisco mania in any case, increased markedly at the end of his life. Graphic and monumental, these late rooms developed into instantly recognizable Michael Taylor trademarks. They also led to the development of the Michael Taylor look-alike school of interior design, a style more suited to sunny, open-air country living than to urban, East Coast life. In Beverly Hills, of course, it went completely haywire.

Actually, the velvet-slippered, old WASP style of society, as nursed along (with varying degrees of success) in many American cities, especially Eastern ones, was anathema to Michael Taylor. He liked Rolls-Royces and gold Rolex watches. The thought of little girls curtsying and parlormaids passing Ritz crackers with bacon and peanut butter in one of his rooms is too silly for words. I don't even think he liked cozy libraries very much. (At least I don't remember ever seeing one he did.) He lived and worked in a town that possessed a stylish social world, one that has always looked down on the vulgarity of Beverly Hills but that still has a lot of Gold Rush sparkle to it. The streets are lined with pretty houses, old *and* new. If anyone wanted to be frumpy and shabby genteel—fine. Michael wasn't going to help them, though. He was in the business of making glamour. One of his jobs of the late sixties that existed until a year ago had two rooms arranged rather like double parlors, one being for dining as well. The colors were all grey and a deep anthracite tone relieved by a considerable amount of gold. French, Italian, and even Portuguese pieces were mixed in a rich but still offhand way. A few tiny slipper chairs were covered in zebra skin. Black urns were stuffed with pheasant feathers. The rooms were seductive and chic.

Twenty years later, Taylor decorated his fourth house for

Michael Taylor's late style was sleek and rough at the same time. The Mimi London tree-trunk table was a trademark.

Mr. and Mrs. Gorham Knowles. Working with the architects Porter & Steinwaddell, whose great talent allows them to combine the Beaux-Arts French attributes typical of so many San Francisco houses with their own more classically informed knowledge of eighteenth-century French architecture, Michael and the Knowleses added to an already beautiful collection of furniture, buying console tables from the Luttrellstown Castle sale, enormous stone garden sculpture, and more antique Chinese wallpaper. The architects installed tall Louis XIV and Louis XV stone chimney breasts and constructed a Herculean stone stairway. On the first floor they constructed a big, skylit garden room that opens off the drawing room, increasing the area for entertaining and at the same time contrasting with the greater formality of the drawing room, with its English rococo console tables and Louis XV armchairs covered in their original needlework. These two very luxurious rooms sum up thirty years of Michael Taylor's decorating philosophy, while still reflecting the owners' tremendous taste. As he added to his considerable range of favorite themes, he continued to retain all his past loves, creating from the influences that had affected him so powerfully a style that was his own. Mimi London says that she is always surprised when people ask who the next Michael Taylor will be. "There won't *be* another Michael." And, of course, she's right.